Working Alone

Working Alone

TIPS & TECHNIQUES for SOLO BUILDING

John Carroll

The Taunton Press

Cover photo: Les Todd

Publisher: Jim Childs
Acquisitions Editor: Steve Culpepper
Assistant Editor: Jennifer Renjilian
Editorial Assistant: Carol Kasper
Copy Editor: Peter Chapman
Designer/Layout Artist: Henry Roth
Illustrator: Scott Bricher
Indexer: Lynda Stannard

The Taunton Press
Inspiration for hands-on living®

Printed in the United States of America
10 9 8 7

The Taunton Press, Inc., 63 South Main Street, PO Box 5506, Newtown, CT 06470-5506
e-mail: tp@taunton.com

Library of Congress Cataloging-in-Publication Data

Carroll, John (John Michael), 1949-
    Working alone : tips & techniques for solo building / John Carroll.
       p. cm.
    Includes index.
    ISBN-13: 978-1-56158-286-0
    ISBN-10: 1-56158-286-7
    1. Building—Technique. 2. House construction—Technique. 3. Self-employed. I. Title.
153.C37   1999
690'.8—dc21   99-33471
                                        CIP

For my son Matthew

Acknowledgments I want to thank four very talented people who have helped bring this book to fruition. First, I'd like to thank Steve Culpepper, who encouraged me to write this book and provided sound guidance through every step of the process. Next, I want to thank the primary editor of this book, Jennifer Renjilian. Jennifer's questions, insights, and suggestions have greatly improved the organization and flow of this book. For providing the fine drawings that appear throughout the book, I'm indebted to Scott Bricher. Finally, I'd like to thank Peter Chapman for copy-editing the book.

About Your Safety

Home building is inherently dangerous. Using hand or power tools improperly or ignoring standard safety practices can lead to permanent injury or even death. Don't try to perform operations you learn about here (or elsewhere) unless you're certain they are safe for you. If something about an operation doesn't feel right, don't do it. Look for another way. We want you to enjoy the craft, so please keep safety foremost in your mind whenever you're building.

CONTENTS

INTRODUCTION   2

CHAPTER 1

Replacing a Helper's Hands   4

The principal challenges of working alone   6
Three ways to overcome the challenges   7

CHAPTER 2

Masonry Work   18

Working with mortar   19
Laying out a foundation   21
Squaring up small projects   32
Setting up scaffolding   33

CHAPTER 3

Floors and Walls   36

Framing floors   37
Building walls   41
Erecting walls   43

CHAPTER 4

Stick-Built Roofs   57

Laying out the roof   58
Building the roof   68

CHAPTER 5

The Shell 77

Framing nonbearing walls 78
Finishing the eaves and rakes 82
Installing windows and doors 88
Shingling the roof 90
Installing wood siding 93

CHAPTER 6

The Interior 98

Hanging drywall 99
Working on doors 103
Running trim 103
Hanging wall cabinets 110
Squaring up a large tile layout 110

CHAPTER 7

Decks 117

Outside structure 118
Inside joists 135
Final steps 139

CHAPTER 8

Limitations of Working Alone 141

Jobs for more than one 142
Using subcontractors to finish the job 145
Facing the workday alone 146

RESOURCES 149
INDEX 151

Introduction

The idea for this book grew out of a casual remark. Several years ago I took a break on a job to chat with the homeowner. "You know," he remarked, "it's really interesting to watch you work. I'm fascinated by the way you manage to hold boards and make measurements by yourself." I'd never given it much thought, but I had, by that time, developed a fairly comprehensive system for working alone.

This system involves a lot of tools and techniques that are not common on building sites and are rarely discussed in books and magazine articles. These methods may be unusual but they are very valuable. Being able to do common building chores alone makes life easier for all kinds of builders—not just self-employed contractors. "Weekend warriors" can do a project without lining up neighbors or in-laws. Professional builders can keep working when some or all of the crew is out. Or they can leave the crew on one job and take care of a small task on another—without dragging along a helper. Even when all hands are present, builders can save time by doing little tasks alone rather than involving a second crew member.

Yet, while the advantages of being able to work alone are easy to see, the techniques themselves are seldom obvious. They sometimes require tools that you're not accustomed to using, and they often require you to alter the pace and the sequence you're used to following. The fact that these techniques aren't immediately apparent, however, doesn't necessarily mean that they're difficult to do. Typically, they only require a different way of approaching your work. I wrote this book to provide that different way of looking at common building problems.

This book is essentially a compilation of the techniques I've developed in my years of working alone. The organization of the chapters follows the schedule of a typical residential building project, but the discussion is not comprehensive by any means. If you're new to this kind of work, use this book in conjunction with a good basic guide (I recommend several at the end of this book). Instead of step-by-step instructions for a specific project, I single out those tasks that are difficult to do alone, then I explain how I approach those tasks by myself. Most of the techniques I describe are fairly easy to understand and accomplish, but some will take time to learn.

Learning any building skill is an active process. To use this book effectively, look carefully at the drawings; think through each problem and try to visualize the solution; and, when you get out on your job, finagle and experiment. Your hands and eyes will teach you the details of these methods. As you work, feel free to disagree with me. The approaches I suggest are, by no means, the last word. On my jobs, I often improvise and experiment, either to solve new problems or to streamline the solutions to old problems. Working alone is a creative process. So, if you see an opportunity to improve a jig or technique I describe, go for it!

You may wonder at times why in the world I don't just hire an assistant. On many occasions, I do just that. In chapter 8, I describe the jobs that I can't or won't do by myself. In lining up subcontractors and temporary helpers, however, I don't take on the responsibility of having a payroll. This simplifies the business end of my company enormously. I do the books for the entire year in one or two days and see an accountant once a year.

Without a crew to keep busy, I always have more work than I can handle. This means I can turn down work that I don't want. Furthermore, by working alone and using a few trusted subcontractors, I'm able to keep a tight lid on my jobs. I work at a manageable pace, make very few mistakes, and don't have to worry about the quality of someone else's work. I rarely get out of sequence or have to redo things. My jobs may not move as quickly as a crew's, but they always move forward. This orderly progress is very satisfying, both to my customers and to me.

I'll never know for sure whether I would make a better living if I had a crew of employees. I do know that I enjoy working alone more. I'm also certain it has made me a better builder. Working alone forces you to set up your jobs more thoroughly and to understand the geometry that your layouts are based on. Because you have to think ahead and schedule tasks more precisely, it hones your planning and management skills. These are valuable skills whether you're working on your own house or running a construction company.

The human hand is a magnificent structure, and it will never be completely replaced. Machines can lift heavier objects; they can work to finer tolerances; they can do repetitive tasks a thousand times faster than human hands. But compared to our hands, they are clumsy and inflexible.

This is readily apparent to those of us who build and repair houses. We use power tools and equipment, but the equipment is portable and guided by our hands. Furthermore, when we use these machines we usually have to finish up by hand. Floor finishers, for example, use sanders to do most of the sanding but follow up with hand tools to do the perimeter of the floor and stair treads. Machines relieve us from a lot of hard, boring work, but they're often too clumsy to finish the job.

Machines are not only clumsy but also expensive and time-consuming. Over the long haul, time and money invested in complex, highly specialized machinery can be recovered on farms and in factories. But on construction sites, which are temporary and ever-changing, it is often impossible to use this kind of equipment effectively or to recover such large capital outlays.

For example, a machine that lays bricks has been around for decades, but it costs hundreds of thousands of dollars and takes days to set up. Such a machine is sometimes used in a factory setting to produce the prefabricated brick panels that go on commercial buildings. But this complex machine is not practical on residential projects where the scale is small, access to the site is often limited, and most of the work can be rapidly completed by skilled craftsmen.

It may seem odd in this age of orchestrated electrons and engineered genes, but the fastest and most cost-effective way to build a house or addition is usually for crews of skilled workers to roll up their sleeves and have at it with portable equipment and handheld tools.

Here's where working alone can get difficult. Those of us in this business cut our eyeteeth as the low man in a crew. We haul boards and bricks, run errands, and get yelled at when we move too slowly. Our principal assets are our hands, and we're reminded of this in the language that's used all through the day. Our bosses tell us to "give me a hand here," "hand me that block," "hold this," "lift that." We grow into our trades in a climate where simple, direct methods are taught and relentless forward progress is demanded.

When you're alone on a job, of course, you don't have the luxury of a helper's hands, so many of the standard techniques are useless. To work alone you develop a different

TRICKS OF THE TRADE

Building Relationships
For jobs that I can't do by myself (I'll talk about these in chapter 8), I hire other self-employed builders to help out for a few hours. These guys are friends, but I don't expect them to work for free. I pay them well for their time so they're encouraged to come back when I need them again. In turn, they call me when they need a hand. And, no matter how hectic my schedule might be, I find time to help them out. They are a vital part of my business.

Handling Emergencies Alone

Because building is an inherently dangerous occupation, it makes sense to be prepared for accidents. Keep a first-aid kit in your car or truck. Also, think about getting a cell phone, which you can keep right beside you as you work. If you're working alone, there's a good chance no one will be around to drive you to a doctor if you get hurt. In these situations, a cell phone may be the most important item to have on site.

mind-set and work at a different pace. You can no longer attack your work as you did when you worked in a crew. This adjustment from a brisk, sometimes frantic pace to a deliberate, measured pace is the first and most important step in becoming an effective solo builder. It's an adjustment that many seasoned builders have a hard time making.

The Principal Challenges of Working Alone

When you decide to take on a project by yourself, you're confronted with two fundamental challenges.

First, how do you measure and mark alone? Measuring and marking by yourself may seem like a daunting challenge. When a helper is on hand, he holds one end of the tape measure or chalkline. But when you're by yourself, you either devise some mechanical means of holding the other end of the tape or line, or you come up with an alternate technique—one that obviates the need for those tools. These methods have to be precise because close measurements are basic to good workmanship. And they have to be fast because you use them often.

The second major challenge is to figure out ways to lift, carry, hold, and align the materials that go into the building. These tasks can be awkward and difficult in some circumstances and dangerous in others. But they don't have to be. In most automotive shops, a single mechanic thinks nothing of removing and replacing an engine that weighs 800 lb. or so. By taking a page or two out of his book, borrowing a couple more from woodworking shops, and stealing the occasional trick from other groups (movers, riggers, sailors, post-and-beam builders, etc.), you can learn to lift and secure just about anything that goes into a house—by yourself.

Three Ways to Overcome the Challenges

Back in the days when I worked in a crew, I sometimes ended up, for one reason or another, alone on a job. In those days I found the situation extremely frustrating. Routine tasks with a helper became slapstick comedies when I was alone, and, true to form, I often took on the role of an exasperated Ollie Hardy or a volcanic Ralph Kramden. I was usually grateful that there were no witnesses to these grim and, no doubt, ridiculous performances.

Today, I'm happy to report, I routinely do all the things by myself that made me look so ridiculous when I was 20 years younger. Although I made this transition gradually (often without consciously thinking about it), I can now identify the three basic ways I was

Installing a Fascia Board

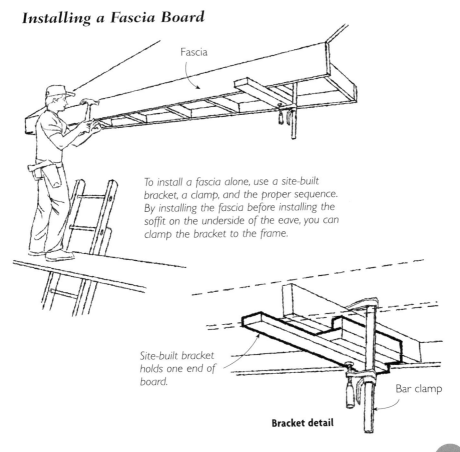

Fascia

To install a fascia alone, use a site-built bracket, a clamp, and the proper sequence. By installing the fascia before installing the soffit on the underside of the eave, you can clamp the bracket to the frame.

Site-built bracket holds one end of board.

Bar clamp

Bracket detail

able to do so. First of all, I've learned to plan and organize my jobs more thoroughly than I did when I had coworkers. Second, I've acquired numerous manufactured tools that help me do without that second pair of hands. And, third, I've become adept at making and using jigs, templates, brackets, and other site-built devices. Although I'll be discussing these approaches separately here, I often use them in combination with each other, as the drawing that shows how I might install a fascia board demonstrates (see p. 7).

Planning to Work Alone

All builders worth their salt develop a well-thought-out master plan at the beginning of a project and a series of battle plans for each phase along the way. Then, as the project gets under way, they come up with modifications in the plan to cover unexpected developments and changes in the design. If you're working alone, you have to do all this planning—and more. You have to include provisions in every phase of the plan for the special problems of doing things with just two hands.

One of the basic planning considerations is the sequence in which you build. As you'll see when we get into specific techniques, there are many instances when you can make your life a lot easier by thinking ahead, anticipating how you're going to do things by yourself, and then coming up with an appropriate order of assembly.

In addition to fine-tuning the sequence of the job, you have to plan just about every step along the way. Often you even have to plan how you're going to do minor chores like safely sawing sheets of plywood or installing long boards. Sometimes these plans require a careful setup or some clever site-built rig. At other times, the plans are focused on subtle aspects of your technique. Starting a nail before you pick up a board, for instance, can make installing that board a lot easier.

see p. 7

TRICKS OF THE TRADE

Using Sharp Hand Tools
As a solo builder, I've found sharp chisels, planes, and handsaws to be an invaluable part of my tool collection. They not only improve the quality of my work but also save steps. Rather than climb down off a scaffold to saw $1/16$ in. off a board, for example, I usually shave it off up on the scaffold with a sharp block plane. It's less work, and I get a better fit in the process.

The Hidden Potential in Manufactured Tools

I spend a lot of time looking at tools and imagining how I'd use them on my jobs. Among builders, this is not terribly unusual behavior. Yet the tools that attract my attention are often quite different from those that interest builders who work in crews. I focus primarily on tools that replace a helper's hands; they're looking for tools that increase productivity and thus help cover the cost of a payroll. But even when a production builder and I have the same tool, we're apt to use it differently. I look for novel uses for common tools; sometimes I see uses for tools that the manufacturers themselves seem to have overlooked.

When I first saw ads in my tool catalogs for Mastodon Jaw Extenders, for example, I knew I had to get a pair. While the manufacturer hawked these devices as a way to make deep clamping affordable, I bought them for a different reason. The 10-in. increase in clamp depth that the Jaw Extenders create when attached to a standard bar or pipe clamp is a great help when I'm clamping something against a wall. With a standard clamp, the handle is too close to the wall to turn, but with the Jaw Extenders attached, the clamp is farther from the wall so I have plenty of room to spin the handle.

Similarly, I recently bought a couple of squares designed for builders who work with steel studs. I hardly ever work with steel studs, but I didn't hesitate to lay down $10 apiece for two of these squares. Called the Swanson Magnetic Square, this tool has magnetic strips that hold the square firmly to steel studs. I wasn't interested in this feature at all, but I could see immediately that the extra-deep (1¼-in.) fence would be very handy for clamping or screwing the square to my work. So as soon as I got the squares home, I drilled several holes in them. Now I can clamp or screw them to the surface of my jobs and use them as brackets for holding up light materials or for anchoring the end of my tape measure.

I've found that tools are often much more versatile than they seem at first. Look at them closely and let your imagination wander—you'll get a lot more out of them.

The process of anticipating problems and then visualizing smooth, effective ways to overcome them is at the heart of working alone. I'll return again and again to this theme as I discuss specific techniques in the chapters that follow.

Using Manufactured Tools

Many of the solutions that I've come up with involve tools and techniques that I rarely, if ever, used when I worked in a crew. Some of the tools are common items that are either ignored or poorly exploited by production crews as they attack their work; others are special-purpose tools that are seldom seen on construction sites (see the sidebar on p. 9).

Clamps and spreaders
I couldn't imagine taking on most of the jobs I do without my large—and growing—collection of clamps. Clamps hold things for me, sometimes for days, and never complain. They serve as handles for carrying sheets of plywood and other unwieldy materials. They provide

Clamps

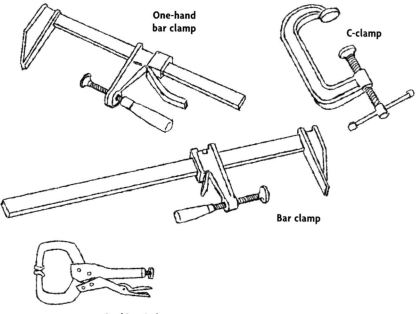

One-hand bar clamp

C-clamp

Bar clamp

Locking C-clamp

muscle to push and pull things into place. And they help make my job sites safe.

C-clamps make the best handles, and they take the place of screws and nails for temporary setups. They're cheap, and they provide plenty of torque, but they're limited in size and aren't good for quick setups. When I need to clamp something larger than 8 in. (the size of my largest C-clamp) I use either a bar clamp or a pipe clamp. My longest bar clamp is 48 in., and my longest pipe clamp is about 72 in. By threading sections of pipe together, however, I've been able to use my pipe clamp for distances of 10 ft. and greater.

When I do a repetitive task, like clamping material at the saw table, I avoid C-clamps. They're frustratingly slow because the only way to adjust them is to turn the threaded bolt. Bar clamps, in contrast, slide quickly into adjustment—the threaded portion is only to apply pressure. Sometimes very little

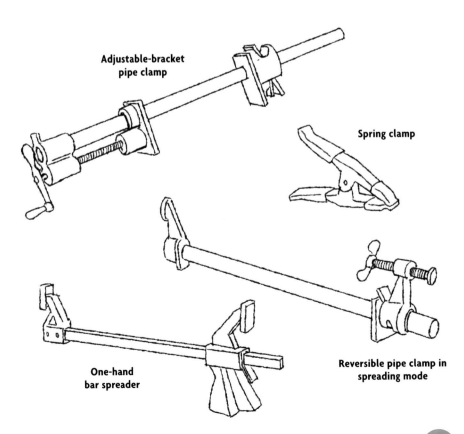

Adjustable-bracket
pipe clamp

Spring clamp

One-hand
bar spreader

Reversible pipe clamp in
spreading mode

pressure is required, though, and a simple spring clamp, which looks and works like a big clothes pin, speeds the process. Another clamp that can be set up and released in a few seconds is the "locking" C-clamp, which uses a cam to apply pressure. These clamps take a minute or so to adjust but provide a lot more pressure than spring clamps and, once adjusted, are quicker than bar clamps. (Unlike bar clamps, which have to be screwed tight each time they're used, locking C-clamps can be tightened with a squeeze of the hand.)

One of the handiest clamps for a solo builder is the one-hand bar clamp. With this kind of clamp, I can position a board with one hand and immediately clamp it in place with the other. One-hand bar clamps aren't cheap, but they're worth the extra expense for the times when you really need them.

By tightening the jaws of a clamp, you can apply hundreds, sometimes thousands, of pounds of squeezing force to the workpiece. Turn the working parts around, and you can apply the same force in the opposite direction. I have two pipe clamps that can be reversed and made into spreaders; and I've also acquired one-hand bar spreaders. I use them mainly for forcing crooked lumber into line.

Sawhorses, scaffolding, and ladders

Large production framing crews often have next to nothing to work off. On many occasions, I've seen carpentry crews spend the day cutting lumber cradled on their foot and working off a single, rickety stepladder and some jerry-built scaffolds. They do a lot of climbing, take unnecessary risks, and squander man-hours, but they usually achieve their primary objective, which is to move rapidly through the project.

A solitary carpenter can't work that way. Because he doesn't have another person to hold boards when he's ripping them or cutting them at an angle, a lone carpenter has to set up a secure sawing station and use clamps (see "Building a Job-Site Sawhorse" on p. 53). And when he starts getting off the ground he needs good, sturdy ladders and scaffolding.

The best all-purpose scaffolding system is pipe scaffolding (the kind bricklayers use). Pipe scaffolding is not terribly expensive, and I've found the six sections I bought years ago to be an excellent investment. If you don't want to buy them, sections of pipe scaffolding can be rented for next to nothing. They're very stable and strong, and, with a little practice, you'll find it

Holding and Fastening a Board by Yourself

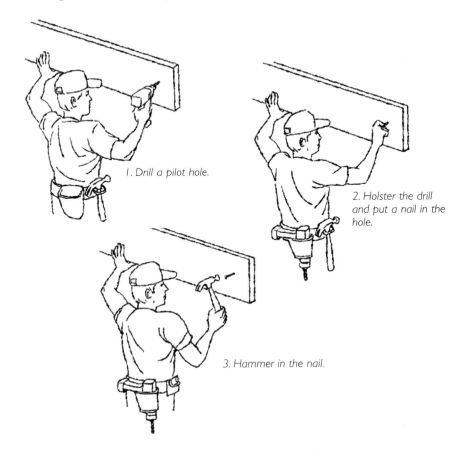

1. Drill a pilot hole.

2. Holster the drill and put a nail in the hole.

3. Hammer in the nail.

easy to set them up and take them down by yourself. (For more on scaffolding, see pp. 33-35.)

When it comes to ladders, I buy only commercial-grade. Factor in the day-to-day aggravation of working with a ladder that doesn't operate smoothly—not to mention the cost of a single visit to the emergency room—and a cheap ladder is a very bad investment.

Fastening options

Holding a board with one hand and nailing it with the other presents a singular challenge. To start the nail, you need two hands—one for the nail and the other for the hammer. If you've got one hand on the board, you've got a problem. In some circumstances, you can get around this problem by using a clamp to hold the board; in others, you can start the nail before you pick up the board. A third option is to have a drill set up with a bit the same diameter as the nails you're using. As you hold the board with one hand, drill a pilot hole with the other (see the drawing on p. 13). Set the drill aside and, using your free hand, slip a nail in the hole. Now grab your hammer and drive the nail home. To do this smoothly, a well-designed tool belt with drill holster and a good cordless drill are highly recommended.

If you're willing to invest a few hundred dollars, there are also two mechanical solutions available. The first is the nail or staple gun. Most of these tools use compressed air to drive the fasteners. Because they can be operated with one hand, holding and fastening a board is a piece of cake. The other one-handed fastening tool is the screw gun.

TRICKS OF THE TRADE

Measuring and Cutting in Place
The best measuring tool is often no measuring tool at all. When possible, simply hold the piece of material in place and mark it directly. In many cases, you don't even have to mark the material. You can often install it long, and then cut it in place.

These are now available with belts of collated screws that feed automatically into the tip of the driver.

Measuring sticks
The standard measuring tool on construction sites is the tape measure. It's accurate, compact, convenient and, as a result, hangs from nearly every tool belt. For the solo builder, however, the tape measure can be a maddening device. It's designed to be pulled, and, as long as it can be hooked or clamped to the work surface, it works great. But when it can't be hooked or affixed at one end, frustration quickly sets in. On flat surfaces, the hook gets in the way and the case repeatedly flops on its side. Over open spaces, the tape collapses.

For a solo worker, it's often a lot easier to use a 6-ft. folding ruler or a measuring stick. I prefer the latter and keep three inexpensive, aluminum rulers—a 24 in., a 48 in., and a 72 in.—on my jobs. Because these lie flat and stay secure on roof decks, floors, and walls, I can effortlessly hold them with one hand while I mark with the other. They're great for measuring across open spaces, and they come in handy as straightedges. I think they're one of the best-kept secrets in building.

Thinking Like a *Gato del Campo*

Years ago, I had a Spanish-speaking employee named Jenaro who, along with other skills, could shape and weld metal. He often showed up at work with special-purpose tools and jigs that he fabricated at home in his spare time. Whenever I asked him where he found the materials for these sundry gadgets, he grinned and said, "los obtuve 'gato del campo,'" by which he meant, "I got them like a country cat." In other words, he scrounged them up by picking through the landfill, foraging at job sites, and getting freebies from coworkers, customers, and unknown citizens who left them at the curbside.

Like Jenaro, I get most of the materials for my jigs and brackets like a country cat. The brackets I use to support siding and trim boards, for example, were originally part of a consumer item designed to provide hooks on the inside of a bathroom door. The bracket draped over the top of a bathroom door, and a rack of hooks for towels, robes, and so on was bolted to it. When one of my less-observant customers asked me to fix his bathroom door, I saw immediately that the brackets were keeping his door from closing properly. By simply removing the brackets and screwing the rack directly to the door, I solved the problem. Then, as I cleaned up the job, I deposited the leftover brackets in my toolbox and, thus, procured another tool like a "gato del campo."

Over the years, I've developed a stray cat's eye for useful discards. I always save large plywood scraps, particularly those from ¾-in. plywood subfloors. From these, I make toolboxes, jigs, and brackets. I also use them as templates, as cutting boards (for cutting insulation), and as knee boards (for finishing concrete).

Other scraps that I always save include long strips ripped from wider boards. From these, I make story poles and measuring sticks. And I never throw away solid-wood doors: Stretched across a pair of sawhorses, these make excellent saw stations. The wide variety of jigs and devices I make have but one feature in common: They all cost exactly what a stray cat pays for a meal.

Using Special-Purpose Tools

Special-purpose tools are made to do one or two things very well. Usually these tools are superbly designed, and they can substantially expand the capabilities and power of the solo builder. In the chapters that follow we'll examine a lift designed specifically for hoisting sheets of drywall, a stand for supporting kitchen cabinets, and a jack for raising framed walls. We'll also look at several special-purpose levers and jacks devoted solely to straightening out crooked lumber. And we'll examine a new breed of builder's level that uses a laser beam and is easily operated by one person. Special-purpose tools are often expensive, but they can clear frustrating, time-devouring obstacles out of the path of a solo builder. The ones I've bought are worth every cent I spent.

However, you can also build your own site-built tools and jigs. Imagine you're working in a 2-ft.-high crawl space, trying to measure the length of each of the bays between the floor joists as you install insulation batts. You're lying on your back, in the dirt, wearing a respirator and working with a very unpleasant material. You definitely don't want this job to drag on any longer than necessary. But every time you extend your tape measure

Using Measuring Sticks

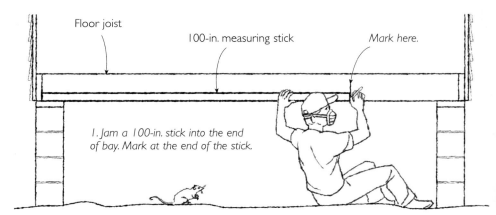

Floor joist

100-in. measuring stick

Mark here.

1. Jam a 100-in. stick into the end of bay. Mark at the end of the stick.

overhead it collapses, which gets frustrating in a hurry.

In such cases, do yourself a favor and leave your tape measure in your toolbox. Instead of fooling with a floppy tape, cut a rigid strip of wood exactly 100 in. long and bring it, along with your store-bought measuring sticks, under the house. To measure a span that's, say, 146½ in. long, jam the 100-in. stick against one end of the bay and mark the joist at the end of the stick (see the drawing below). Then measure the remaining 46½ in. by jamming a store-bought measuring stick against the other end. You can use the same tools to measure and then to cut the insulation. They also make good weapons if you're approached by unfriendly vermin.

The 100-in. measuring stick is but one of dozens of site-built tools and jigs I use to work safely and smoothly by myself. Most of these are easy to put together, can be saved for future projects, and—this is the part I really like—cost nothing but the little time I put into them.

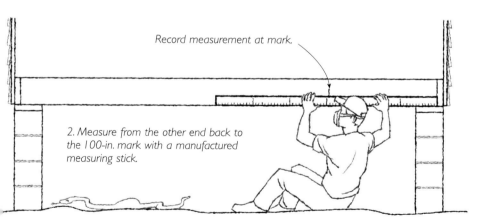

Record measurement at mark.

2. Measure from the other end back to the 100-in. mark with a manufactured measuring stick.

MASONRY WORK

If you have the skills and are willing to endure the plodding pace, there are no serious obstacles to laying brick and block alone. Bricks and blocks are manufactured in sizes that can be easily handled by one person. Mortar can be mixed in small batches and then placed in the structure one trowelful at a time, although keeping mortar fresh does present some challenges to a solo builder. Except for concrete, which I'll discuss in chapter 8, virtually all masonry materials can be moved, lifted, and installed by one person without undue difficulty.

The main challenge in masonry work is not in the installation, it's in the layout, particularly the layout of broad structures like foundations. Laying out a foundation is difficult enough for a crew of two or three; for a solo worker, it can seem like an insurmountable task. Because of several difficulties with measuring and because the layout has to be precise in three dimensions, perfectly level, and at the correct height, I do not lay out whole house foundations by myself (see chapter 8 for more on the reasons why). However, I have laid out the foundations for large additions by myself, and I've worked out a system that is precise and takes a reasonable amount of time (about four hours for a simple rectangular addition).

Building the masonry structures is not difficult for one person—either at ground level or above. But because of the weight of masonry materials, building above ground level does call for scaffolding. With the right techniques and some planning, it's possible for one person to erect the scaffolding and make it level.

Working with Mortar

When most people look at a brick wall they see bricks; when a mason looks at a brick wall he sees mortar. The reason for this is simple:

The quality and craftsmanship of brick structures are determined primarily by the mortar. When it's installed properly, mortar holds bricks tenaciously together and seals out water. And it's pleasing to the eye—well-crafted brick walls have mortar joints that are neat and consistent in size, color, and tooling.

The key to getting this kind of workmanship is to use mortar that is mixed just right. Getting the dry ingredients correctly proportioned is a simple matter. The Portland Cement Association recommends mixing $2\frac{1}{2}$ to 3 parts sand to 1 part masonry cement. To do this, I fill the same bucket $2\frac{1}{2}$ times with sand, followed by 1 bucketful of masonry cement. If I want to make a small batch of mortar, I use a 1-gal. bucket or even a coffee can. If I want to make a large batch, I use a 5-gal. bucket.

Determining the amount of water needed is not so simple. Here the Portland Cement Association does not suggest a proportion; instead it recommends that the mortar should be as wet as possible—to achieve a strong bond—yet have enough body to let the mason do good, neat work. Because the moisture content of the sand varies, the amount of water needed to make good, workable mortar changes from day to day. Thus there is no

Installing
Flue Liners
If you don't happen to have the digital strength of a rock climber, it's very difficult to hold the larger sizes of flue liners between your fingers as you lower them into place. You can make this job a lot easier by affixing two C-clamps at the top opening of the liner before you pick it up. The clamps serve as handles as you lower the flue into position during installation.

ing is not only time-consuming, but it also affects the strength of the mortar. As a result, the Portland Cement Association recommends discarding unused mortar after 2 hours.

Without question, the best way to lay bricks is to use fresh mortar. So it makes sense to mix up just enough for 1 to 2 hours of work. This requires careful planning—particularly when you're working alone. I try to get everything into position—the bricks, the blocks, the line, and the tools—before I make the mortar. I also size the batch according to how fast I think I'll use it. If I'm building a foundation, I make a large batch because I know I'll go through the mortar quickly. If I'm building a chimney, on the other hand, I make smaller batches because the work goes slower.

formula for the correct amount of water to use, and masons simply add water until the mix looks and feels right.

Making a perfect batch of mortar doesn't mean that it will stay that way. All cement-based products begin changing the moment they're mixed with water. To maintain a good workable consistency, masons sometimes "retemper" the mortar by mixing in small amounts of water. In this regard, they can go to the well only so many times. The longer a batch of mortar sits in the pan, the harder it is to work with and the more frequently it has to be retempered. Excessive retemper-

When I'm working off a scaffold, I mix smaller batches than when I'm working on ground level because I know that hauling the mortar up a ladder one bucketful at a time will slow me down. If I'm building an arch and I know I'll have a lot of time-consuming cuts to make, I do as much of the cutting as I can before I mix the mortar. And because such work goes very slowly, I mix a very small batch.

Laying Out a Foundation

When I lay out any foundation, I have two basic concerns. First, I want to get the layout level and at the right elevation or height. Second, I want to get the foundation square and to the right length and width. To accomplish the first goal, I use a laser level to establish the top surface of the foundation. To accomplish the second goal, I use careful measurements and geometry to lay out the length and width of the foundation. When I'm done, the layout consists of several strings set up to represent the precise, outside dimensions of the foundation. These strings serve as references to measure against as I build the foundation.

Establishing the Level Plane

To illustrate how I go about laying out the foundation for an addition, I'll walk through the steps for a foundation that's 20 ft. 8 in. long and 12 ft. wide. The steps are the same for any size addition foundation. For distances less than 30 ft. (the length of my basic tape measure), I've found that using inches simplifies mathematical calculations. So, I'll refer to this as a 248-in. by 144-in. foundation.

The long wall

After stripping the siding off the house, I need to make two marks exactly 248 in. apart on the exposed frame of the house. These marks represent the long dimension of the foundation. Making the first mark is easy: The addition typically begins at or a few feet from the corner of the house or some other critical reference (such as a door).

Pulling the 248-in. measurement and making the second mark is the hard part. Because no helpers are available, I need to rig up some way to hold the end of the tape as I pull it out and mark the 248-in. dimension. To do this, I nail a scrap of 2x2 to the wall with the end of it even with my first mark; then I hook my tape over the end of the scrap, pull the measurement, and make the second mark (see the drawing on p. 22). Once in a while the hook of the tape slips off the end of the block. When this happens, I use a spring clamp to hold it to the block.

Once the long ends of the foundation are marked on the house, it's time to lay out the long, outside wall of the foundation that runs parallel to and 144 in. away from the house. I begin this process by driving four 2x4 stakes into the ground. I install these stakes in pairs a few feet outside the marks on the house that represent the new foundation. I put one stake in each pair roughly 120 in. away from the house, and the other

Pulling a Wall Measurement

A scrap of wood nailed to the side of the house provides a surface to hook your tape measure to. If the tape slips off the block of wood, clamp it in place.

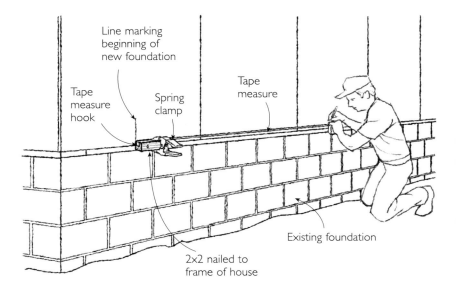

Line marking beginning of new foundation

Tape measure hook

Spring clamp

Tape measure

Existing foundation

2×2 nailed to frame of house

about 160 in. away. (Because this is a rough measurement, I run my tape measure along the ground and don't worry about hooking it to the building.) This way the stakes straddle a line parallel to and 144 in. away from the house. Because I will mark the top of the foundation on these stakes, I make sure that their tops are higher than the foundation of the house.

With the stakes in place, I'm ready to set up my laser level. I usually set the laser up inside the foundation I'm laying out, but because it

has an effective range of 100 ft., I can set it up just about any place inside or near the new foundation. Builders use several tools to accurately mark off a level plane, but when you're working alone nothing is easier to use than a laser level. For me, this tool has been a great investment, and I highly recommend it to anyone who does a lot of solo building.

Properly adjusted, my laser level emits a level laser beam that's accurate within a ¼ in. over 100 ft. When I rotate the instrument, this

Marking the Top of the Foundation

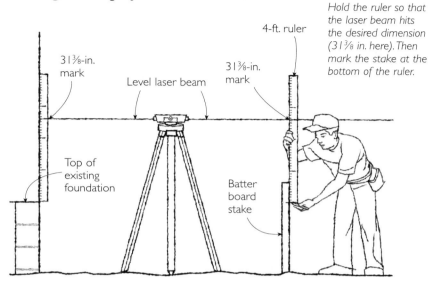

4-ft. ruler

Hold the ruler so that the laser beam hits the desired dimension (31⅜ in. here). Then mark the stake at the bottom of the ruler.

31⅜-in. mark

Level laser beam

31⅜-in. mark

Top of existing foundation

Batter board stake

After leveling the instrument, measure the difference in elevation (31⅜ in. here) between the laser beam and the top of the foundation. Then measure down the same amount at each stake to transfer the top-of-foundation elevation to the stakes.

beam becomes, in effect, a level plane about 200 ft. wide. As you'll see, this plane serves as a reference to measure against when I lay out the top of my foundations.

The first step is to carefully adjust the instrument so it remains level no matter which direction I point it in. Then I aim it at the house. The laser beam shows up as a red dot, about ⅛ in. wide, on the side of the house. Next I measure the distance between the center of this dot and the top of the existing foundation, known as the "differ-

ence in elevation." For this foundation, the distance is 31⅜ in. I use this difference in elevation to transfer the elevation of the top of the foundation from the house to the stake.

I point the laser level at each stake and measure down 31⅜ in. from the laser dot with a 48-in. measuring stick. To get the measurement, I hold the ruler vertically and move it up or down until the laser dot centers on the 31⅜-in. mark. Then I mark the stake at the bottom of the ruler.

When all four stakes are marked, I clamp a 2x4 batter board horizontally across each pair of stakes so the top of the board aligns with the marks on the stake. To get the top edge of each batter board exactly even with the marks, I hold the board precisely in place with one hand while I clamp it with the other, using a large spring clamp. (I could also use a one-hand bar clamp or a locking C-clamp.) After the batter boards are in place, I add C-clamps to hold the batter boards securely for the week or two that I need to leave them in place.

Laying Out the Length and Width

Once the batter boards are level and at the same height as the top of the house foundation, it's time to set a string across them that is parallel to and precisely 144 in. away from the existing foundation wall. To have something to hook the tape on as I make this measurement, I nail a short piece of 2x4 to the house. Before nailing it to the house, though, I cut a rectangular block out of it so that it ends up roughly L-shaped. Then I use a chisel to make a slight recess in the back side of the horizontal

Laying Out the Long Wall

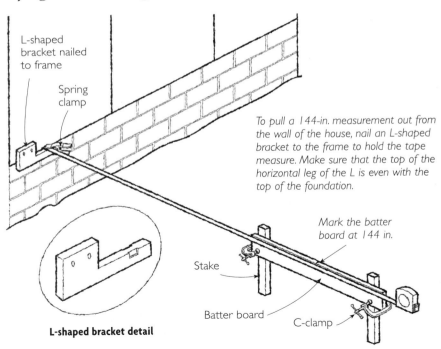

L-shaped bracket nailed to frame

Spring clamp

To pull a 144-in. measurement out from the wall of the house, nail an L-shaped bracket to the frame to hold the tape measure. Make sure that the top of the horizontal leg of the L is even with the top of the foundation.

Mark the batter board at 144 in.

Stake

Batter board

C-clamp

L-shaped bracket detail

leg of the L. When I nail this bracket to the house, I set it so that the top of the cut-out portion is even with the top of the foundation.

The slight recess allows me to insert the hook of the tape in the crack between the house and the bracket. To hold the tape in place, I use a spring clamp. I pull the tape measure out from the house and mark the batter board at 144 in. After doing this on both ends of the foundation, I set up the string on the batter boards running from mark to mark.

To hold the string on the batter boards, I use mason's line blocks. The advantage of these blocks is that I can slide them laterally along the batter board as I fine-tune the position of the string in relation to the house. Chances are I haven't pulled the initial 144-in. measurement precisely perpendicular to the house, so the string will not be exactly 144 in. from the house. To get the string exactly 144 in. from the house, I swing the tape measure in a gentle arc (see the drawing below). When the tape measure is at the high point in the arc, it is

Pulling a Perpendicular Measurement

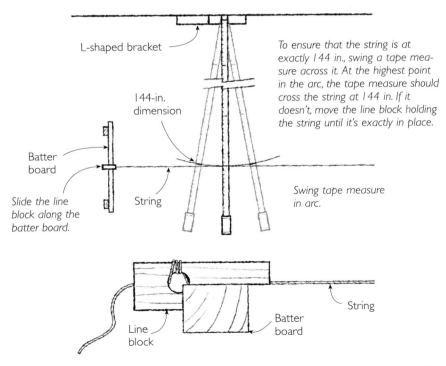

L-shaped bracket

144-in. dimension

Batter board

Slide the line block along the batter board.

String

To ensure that the string is at exactly 144 in., swing a tape measure across it. At the highest point in the arc, the tape measure should cross the string at 144 in. If it doesn't, move the line block holding the string until it's exactly in place.

Swing tape measure in arc.

String

Line block

Batter board

Math and the Solo Builder

The first time I ever "squared up" a foundation, I was working with a crew. We set up two parallel pairs of strings representing the length and width of the foundation. Then we measured the diagonals of the layout, which, predictably, were unequal. To get them equal, we shifted the position of the side walls down the length of one of the long-wall strings. Working systematically, we moved and measured the strings until the diagonals of the layout were exactly even—at which point we knew we had a true rectangle.

This method was gratifyingly simple, and the whole process took no more than 15 minutes. Unfortunately, it's just about impossible for one person to square up a foundation this way. Other trial-and-error techniques used at different stages of construction are similarly difficult for the solo builder to use. So we come face-to-face with one of the inescapable facts of working alone: You usually can't use the empirical, trial-and-error techniques that generations of builders have devised. You need another way, and that way is the math that you learned—or were supposed to have learned—in high school.

Using math doesn't necessarily mean doing math. You can use a construction calculator, which provides the diagonal of the foundation after you punch in the length and width. Some builders love this gadget, but don't be fooled into thinking it's essential. In 30 years of building I've never needed a construction calculator. Using a basic $6 calculator and the geometry I took in high school, I can find the hypotenuse of any right triangle in less than a minute.

In the final analysis, though, it doesn't really matter whether you use a construction calculator or a basic calculator to help you solve building problems. The important thing is that you use the math. It's a valuable tool that doesn't require a helper, is accurate, and saves time. Even when you have a second pair of hands available, it doesn't make sense to spend 15 minutes searching by trial-and-error for a measurement you can compute in seconds. Math is a vital tool when you're working alone, and, because it saves time and reduces physical exertion, it makes you a better builder when you're working in a crew.

at the true 144-in. dimension. While holding the tape measure at this point, slide the line to the 144-in. dimension when it reaches the high point in the arc.

I repeat this process at each end of the foundation until I'm certain the string is parallel to and 144 in. away from the wall of the house. When I'm satisfied with the final position of the string, I mark it clearly on the batter boards, remove the line blocks, and install screws at the marks. Then I stretch a string from screw to screw; this string represents the top, outside edge of the long wall of the new foundation.

The short walls

As soon as I get the line representing the long wall precisely into position, I'm ready to lay out the two short, perpendicular walls. The position of both walls in relation to the house was already established when I made the two marks on the house 248 in. apart. The mission now is to lay out the outboard end of those walls and mark exactly where they will intersect with the long wall.

It's essential to get these walls precisely perpendicular to the long walls. To do this I use an old and reliable tool—a tool developed in the 6th century B.C. by the Greek mathematician, Pythagoras. That tool is the Pythagorean Theorem, perhaps the most useful theorem in all of mathematics for builders. The Pythagorean Theorem holds that "the square of the length of the hypotenuse of a right triangle is equal to the sum of the squares of

The Pythagorean Theorem

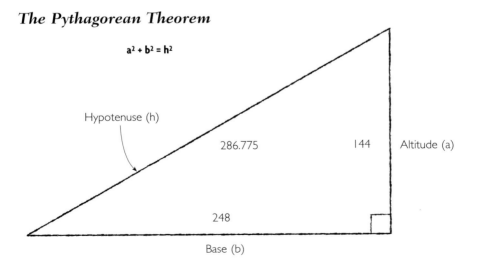

$$a^2 + b^2 = h^2$$

Hypotenuse (h)

286.775

144   Altitude (a)

248

Base (b)

the lengths of the legs (altitude and base)," which I know sounds confusing. Fortunately, it can be reduced to a formula that is easy to use:

$$a^2 + b^2 = h^2$$

In most cases, you'll know the dimensions of the altitude and base (**a** and **b**) of the triangle because they will be existing dimensions on your layout (they are the short and long foundation measurements in our example). Plug those dimensions into the Pythagorean Theorem to find **h**. With the length

of the hypotenuse in hand, you can quickly lay out a right triangle. If the hypotenuse is correctly computed and all three sides of the triangle are accurately measured, the altitude and base (**a** and **b**) will be precisely perpendicular to each other. Now, let's apply this math to our foundation example.

When I start the math process, I know the lengths of the altitude and base—they are the width and length of the foundation, or 144 in. and 248 in., respectively. To find the hypotenuse, I plug those numbers into the Pythagorean Theorem as follows:

$$a^2 + b^2 = h^2$$

$$144^2 + 248^2 = h^2$$

$$82{,}240 = h^2$$

$$\sqrt{82{,}240} = h$$

$$286.775 \text{ or } 286\tfrac{3}{4} = h$$

Pulling the length of the hypotenuse ($286\tfrac{3}{4}$ in.) diagonally across the layout from each side and marking where that dimension intersects with the string establishes the point of intersection of the altitude (the side wall in this case) and hypotenuse of the right triangle (see the drawing on p. 31). Barring a sudden change in the rules of geometry, I know that if the side

(see the drawing on p. 31).

TRICKS OF THE TRADE

Converting from Decimals to Fractions

To convert the decimal portion of an inch to sixteenths, multiply by 16. The resulting number, after rounding, is the number of sixteenths. For example, for a measurement of 286.775 in., multiply the decimal portion, 0.775, by 16. Round the answer, 12.4, to 12. So 0.775 = $^{12}/_{16}$, which is ¾. To convert quarters, eighths, or sixteenths to decimals, simply divide the numerator (the upper number) by the denominator (the lower number). To convert $^{13}/_{16}$ to a decimal, for example, divide 13 by 16. This comes to 0.8125.

A Bracket for Diagonal Measurements

You can overcome the biggest challenge of laying out an addition foundation—pulling the diagonal measurement to square up the layout—by fabricating a bracket to hold the tape at the correct angle.

Step 1
On a piece of scrap plywood lay out a scaled drawing of the foundation and mark the hypotenuse. Then measure the angle between the hypotenuse and altitude to find out the angle at which you need to hold the tape.

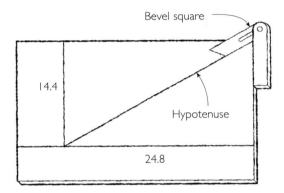

Bevel square

14.4

Hypotenuse

24.8

Step 2
Transfer the angle to an L-shaped bracket.

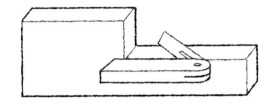

Step 3
Cut a kerf in the bracket where you've marked the angle. Then insert the hook of the tape measure into the kerf and you are ready to measure the diagonal.

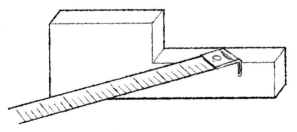

walls meet the outside wall at this point, then they will be perpendicular to the long walls.

With a helper, pulling these measurements takes just a few minutes. If I'm by myself, however, it takes about 20 minutes. That's because I not only have to come up with a way to hold the end of the tape measure precisely in place, but I also have to hold it at the right angle for a diagonal measurement.

To determine the angle, I make a scaled drawing that duplicates the angle of the hypotenuse I need to pull. A plywood scrap works well for this purpose because it typically has a nice, square, factory-cut corner. From the corner of the scrap, I measure 14.4 in. up along the vertical edge and 24.8 in. out along the bottom edge. By connecting these two marks with a straightedge, I create an accurate scaled drawing exactly one-tenth as big as the full-sized triangle I want to lay out. (The full-sized layout is 144 in. by 248 in.) For making one-tenth scaled drawings like these, I use the 10ths scale on my rafter square.

The line I drew connecting the marks is the hypotenuse of my miniature triangle. The angle of this line in relation to the base of the triangle, therefore, is the exact same angle (in relation to the wall of the house) that I need to pull my diagonal measurement. But because the hook of the tape runs perpendicular across its length I scribe a line running perpendicular to the hypotenuse of the miniature triangle with a rafter square. I measure the angle formed by this line and the base of the triangle with a bevel square. Then I transfer this angle (which is about a 30° bevel) to an L-shaped bracket, as shown in the drawing on p. 29. This angle, incidentally, is the same as the angle formed by the altitude and the hypotenuse, and you can save time by simply measuring the angle there after you've drawn the scaled right triangle.

This process is a lot to go through for two measurements. But the measurements have to be accurate because they render the foundation —and hence the entire addition— square. Making the scaled drawing doesn't take more than 5 minutes. (I just did it in 3 minutes.) If this process is intimidating, you can try a couple of other approaches. Try calculating the angle, which is the equivalent of the plumb cut on a rafter, using algebra or trig. To use algebra to convert the width and length of this foundation into roof pitch, the math would look like this:

$$144/248 = x/12$$

$$144/248 = 6.97/12$$

Overview of Layout

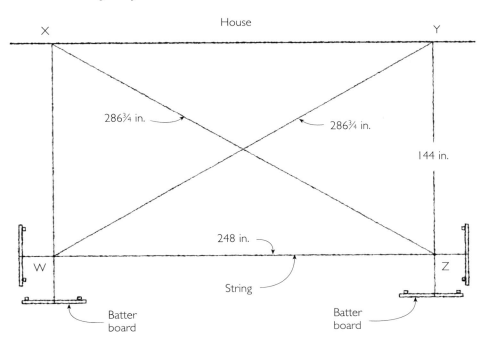

Use a Swanson Speed Square or a Stanley Quick Square to lay out the plumb cut of a 7-in-12 rafter. That's the angle you need for the kerf. To find the angle using trigonometry, divide the width of the foundation by the length, then multiply the result by tan^{-1}. The math looks like this:

$$144/248 \times \tan^{-1} = 30.1°$$

Use a Swanson Speed Square or a Stanley Quick Square to lay out a 30° bevel angle for the kerf.

After marking the angle on the L-shaped bracket, I use a handsaw to cut a kerf about ½ in. deep along the angled line. Then I nail the L-shaped bracket to the wall so that the top of the horizontal leg of the L is even with the top of the foundation and the inside edge of the kerf intersects with the end-of-foundation mark on the wall.

To measure the diagonal of the foundation, I insert the hook of my tape measure in the kerf, hold it in place with a spring clamp, and pull the tape diagonally across the layout to the string that indicates the long outside wall. I mark the string with a felt-tipped marker where the 286¾-in. measurement intersects with the string (point Z on the drawing on p. 31). After repeating this process across the other diagonal of the layout (point W), I've got two marks on the string that represent the two outside corners of the foundation.

To check my work, I always measure from dot to dot along the line and make sure that distance is the same as the length of the layout (248 in., in this case). Because there is nothing at either dot to hook to, I pull the measurement from one of the batter boards, note the amount at the first dot, then continue pulling to the second dot. By subtracting the first measurement from the second, I get the dot-to-dot measurement. After I determine that the layout is correct (within ½ in. of square), I set up batter boards to hold the strings representing the side walls.

By stretching a string that runs from the mark on the house (point Y) through the mark on the string (point Z) to a batter board, I lay out the top outside edge of the right side wall. The process is the same for the left side wall, with the string going from point X though point W.

Squaring Up Small Projects

Laying out the base of masonry structures with a small footprint (chimneys, porches, steps, and so on) is a lot easier than laying out the broad foundations that support houses and additions. To square up really small jobs, I just use my rafter square. For jobs wider than 30 in., I often use a sheet of plywood as a square. The factory-cut end is usually within ⅛ in. of being square to the long side. When I don't have a sheet of plywood handy or the layout is wider than 5 ft., I use geometry to calculate the hypotenuse (or diagonal), as just described in the previous section. Then I measure that dimension with a measuring stick, which is a lot easier than using a tape measure.

For long, narrow projects, it's not necessary to calculate and measure the diagonal of the entire layout. To lay out a 6-ft. by 24-ft. porch, for example, I prefer to block off a 6-ft. square at each end of the layout (see the drawing on the facing page). I use the diagonal of that square to get the side walls of the porch perpendicular. This technique allows me to use a measuring stick for the diagonal measurement instead of fabricating a bracket to hold the end of the tape.

To create the triangle, I attach a string to batter boards centered 6 ft.

Squaring the Sides of a Long, Narrow Addition

Block off a square section at each end of the layout and calculate the hypotenuse. The 101¹³⁄₁₆-in. measurement can then be measured with a measuring stick made from a strip of wood.

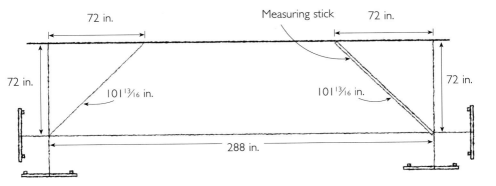

from the house and outside the foundation. I measure in 6 ft. from each end of the layout marks on the house. I calculate the hypotenuse of a right triangle with both sides 72 in. long (6 ft. converted to inches). The Pythagorean Theorem works for this calculation, but there's a faster way. The formula for finding the hypotenuse of a right triangle with two equal sides (or the diagonal of a square) is 1.414 x the length of one side. That number is hard to remember, but it's actually the square root of 2, which is easier to remember. So to get the hypotenuse for our layout triangles, the equation is:

$$\sqrt{2} \times 72 = 101.82$$

This process requires five keystrokes and takes less than 15 seconds. So, it's well worth learning if you're not already familiar with it. With the hypotenuse measurement I can now mark where the walls of the addition should be, and I know they will be perpendicular.

Setting Up Scaffolding

If you work systematically, you can set up and take down pipe scaffolding safely and efficiently by yourself. A section of pipe scaffolding consists of two end frames and two cross braces (see the drawing on p. 34). Before I begin assembling the bottom section of scaffolding, I insert four leveling feet into the

A Section of Scaffolding

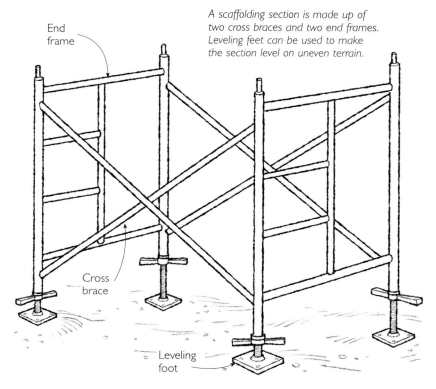

End frame

A scaffolding section is made up of two cross braces and two end frames. Leveling feet can be used to make the section level on uneven terrain.

Cross brace

Leveling foot

bottom legs of the two end frames. I set two braces where I can reach them as I stand up the first end frame. Holding the end frame with one hand, I slip the braces onto the toggle pins of the frame with the other. With the braces in place, I can leave the first end frame upright but leaning at an angle while I fetch the second end frame. When I attach the second end frame to the braces, the first section of scaffolding is assembled and in the right place.

To level the assembly, I determine which end frame is the higher of the two. I clamp my level to the top bar of that end frame and raise the leg on the low side by rotating the threaded bracket on the leveling foot. Leveling feet are not absolutely necessary (you can raise the lower side of the end frame by setting scraps of wood under the leg), but they are very convenient. I recommend renting or buying these leveling feet whenever you have to use this kind of scaffolding.

After I get the first end frame level, I place my level on a straight board that bridges both end frames, and bring the second end frame up level with the first.

Once I get the first section nice and level, I set a few scaffolding boards across the top and lean two end frames and two braces against the standing section of scaffolding so I'll be able to reach them from the first level. Then I climb up on top of the boards and pull the end frames up one at a time and set them over the pins in the end frames below.

After both end frames are in place, I install the braces. Trying to install this second tier of end frames from the ground is a direct approach that, at first, seems like the natural way to go. But when you hold the end frame upright from the bottom, you surrender a serious mechanical advantage. It's much easier and safer to work with gravity and lower the end frame into place from above. I never begrudge the time it takes to climb up on the scaffold because I know I'll have to get up there anyway to install the braces.

To erect subsequent layers of scaffolding, repeat the process, setting scaffolding boards in place then installing each end frame from above. I leave the boards in place

Scaffold Height *Scaffolding that is over three sections high should always be attached to the house to prevent it from tipping over. To connect the scaffold to the house, I attach a scrap of 2x4 to the house, screw the brace to the scrap, then attach the scaffold to the brace with metal pipe straps. These are rigid and fit snugly over the round bars of the scaffold end frames. I use screws throughout this operation, both because they hold better than nails and because they're easier to remove when I take down the scaffolds.*

as I move up, both because I need something to stand on to safely install each new section of boards and because I'll need to have something to stand on later when I take the scaffolding down. When I get above the third tier of scaffolding, I use a rope to pull the end frame up; later, when I'm taking down the scaffold, I use the rope to lower the pieces to the ground.

When you finish the foundation and turn your attention to the frame, you confront a new and very different set of problems as a solo builder. Happily, though, this phase of the job begins not over uneven ground but on a square and level surface—the top of the foundation. This not only provides a tangible reference to measure against and a level base to build on, but it also gives you something to hook or clamp your tape measure to.

These very real advantages should not be overstated, however. Laying out the various parts of the frame is a big job, and there are hundreds of measurements involved for most residential frames, some of which are quite difficult for a person working alone to do.

Yet the layout is not nearly as difficult as the second basic challenge that solo builders face: moving, lifting, and installing framing materials. In contrast to the compact and easy-to-manage masonry units that make up the foundation, the solo builder is now faced with boards that are 12 ft., 16 ft., even 20 ft. long, and sheets of plywood that are 4 ft. across and 8 ft. long. To compound the problems (literally), it's often convenient or necessary to combine these materials into larger components before lifting them into place.

The materials of the frame are not only large and unwieldy, but they are also far from perfect. Wood products are, by their nature, dimensionally unstable. By the time builders get their hands on them, wood is often cupped, bowed, or twisted. Seasoned carpenters expect these flaws and respond by culling the worst specimens and by pushing, pulling, torquing, and levering the others into a reasonably straight line as they install them. This process is not too difficult when two or three carpenters are working together, but when a carpenter works alone it takes some unique thought and effort.

Framing Floors

Floor systems span across open spaces and have to support the weight of partitions and finish materials as well as the people and furnishings that will eventually go inside the house. Because of these requirements, floor systems have to be built out of substantial pieces of wood. There is no such thing as a standard floor system, but a typical system on my jobs consists of a framework made out of 2x10s and a deck comprised of ¾-in. tongue-and-groove plywood. This wood is heavy, and lifting and carrying it is hard work. Yet this part of the job is not nearly as challenging as getting the individual pieces of wood, which are invariably warped, bowed, or imperfect in any of a dozen other ways, joined together in a reasonably straight, plumb, and square structure.

Laying Out the Floor System

If you're working alone, laying out the floor system of a house or addition presents few serious obstacles. A minor problem that occurs right at the beginning is when you have to transfer the location of the anchor bolts (which are sticking out of the top of the foundation) onto the mudsill. To mark them, carpenters usually set the sill on top of the foundation, push it against the bolts, and transfer the location of the bolts with a square.

Laying Out Bolt Locations on the Mudsill

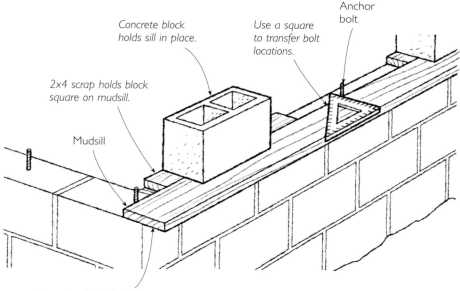

Concrete block holds sill in place.

Use a square to transfer bolt locations.

Anchor bolt

2x4 scrap holds block square on mudsill.

Mudsill

More than half of the mudsill is off the edge of the foundation.

The problem for a solo builder is that the sill usually has to be held in this position because less than half its width is sitting on top of the wall. To keep the sill from falling, I set a couple of concrete blocks on it. Putting a scrap of 2x4 under one side of the block holds it square with the top of the foundation, as shown in the drawing above. Once the bolt locations are marked, it's a simple matter to drill the holes and bolt the mudsill in place.

When it's time to lay out the joist locations, another measuring technique is useful. To get the layout 16 in. on center (o.c.), I usually mark at 15¼ in., then pull the tape measure from that point, marking every 16 in. and setting the X ahead of the marks (see the drawing on the facing page). This technique allows the first full sheet of plywood to break evenly on the joists. To provide something at the 15¼-in. mark to hook the tape measure to, I nail my square to the sill at the mark. I've drilled two holes through my square just for this purpose.

Wrestling the Wood into Place

As I install the floor system, I use a variety of tools to straighten the

Laying Out Joist Locations

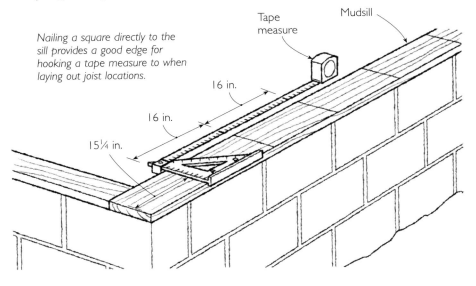

Nailing a square directly to the sill provides a good edge for hooking a tape measure to when laying out joist locations.

Tape measure

Mudsill

16 in.

16 in.

15¼ in.

wood (see the drawing on p. 40). To straighten twisted joists as I attach them to the band joist (also called the rim joist), I use a tool designed specifically for this purpose, called the Tweaker, which is an h-shaped steel bar. I begin this process by attaching the bottom of the joist on the layout line. Then I hook the Tweaker over the top edge of the joist. Holding the tool in my left hand, I lever the joist into line as I nail through the band joist and into the top of the joist end with my right hand. If I'm not using a nail gun, of course, I have to start the nail before I grab the Tweaker.

If necessary, I repeat the process at the other end of the joist.

Attaching both ends of the joists at the layout lines does not guarantee that the midspans of the joists are on layout. More often than not, the joists are bowed and I have to pull or push them into the 16-in. o.c. layout as I nail the plywood subfloor. To do this, I use either a bar clamp (for pulling) or a spreader (for pushing) that I set perpendicularly across the top of the joists.

The most difficult part of the floor system to install solo is tongue-

Tools for Working the Wood

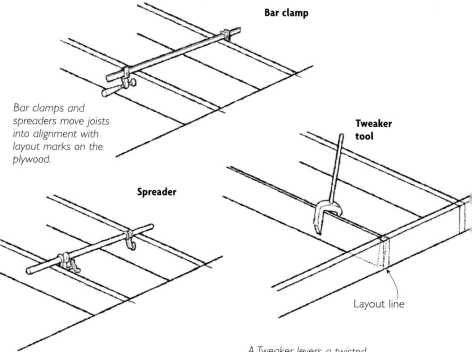

Bar clamp

Bar clamps and spreaders move joists into alignment with layout marks on the plywood.

Tweaker tool

Spreader

Layout line

A Tweaker levers a twisted joist to the layout line.

and-groove plywood decking. Getting the tongue in the groove is the rub. The plywood rarely lies flat, so it's necessary to force it down against the joists as you drive it into the adjoining pieces. When you have a crew handy, all you have to do is station a well-fed helper to weigh down the side where the new sheet engages the previous row. Then you use a sledgehammer to knock the new sheet into the groove of the previously installed sheets.

Working alone, of course, you don't have access to such a partner, so you need an alternate way to get the sheet flat. One way is to use hold-down blocks. First, lay the sheet in place about ¼ in. from the previously installed sheets. Then, while standing on the new sheet, screw two or three blocks of wood on top of the previous row so they overhang the joist where the next sheet goes. The blocks hold the new sheet in line as you drive it into place with a sledge.

Protecting the Decking *To protect the outside edge of plywood decking as you bang it into place, use a "beating block." The ideal material for this sacrificial layer is a strip of the decking itself. Find a scrap with the factory-cut tongue and cut a strip about 4 in. wide and 48 in. long. Tap the tongue of the strip into the grooved edge of the plywood, then pound away with your sledgehammer. If you don't have a scrap of the decking handy, use a straight strip of 2x4.*

This technique works fairly well, but I've found that using a special-purpose tool, called a BoWrench, works even better. The BoWrench is a large steel lever hinged at one end to an F-shaped bar. To use the tool, I hook the arms of the F over a joist just beyond the sheet and pull the plywood into place, as shown in the drawing on p. 42. The long handle provides plenty of leverage and allows me to kneel on the mating edge of the plywood as I pull it into place. My own weight holds the sheet flat, so I don't have to install and later take up the hold-down blocks. Also, because I'm not banging the edge of the plywood, the chance of damaging

the groove—and thus making the job more difficult when I install the next row of plywood—is greatly reduced. The BoWrench and the Tweaker are both excellent special-purpose tools with painless price tags; I strongly recommend them for anyone who does a lot of solo building.

Building Walls

The process of laying out and building walls is quite manageable for one person, and even when a full crew is available it makes sense to divide much of the labor into individual tasks. In this section, I'll describe a few simple techniques I've developed to help lay out and build walls without a helper. These solo techniques should not be reserved for those occasions when you're on a job by yourself, though. They are quick and accurate, and they often require less time than it would take to get a coworker to stop what he's doing to give you a hand.

Laying Out the Walls

The only purpose of the second person at layout stage is to hold the end of the tape measure, and it's not that difficult to find a mechanical means to do that. Laying out the walls by yourself not only frees the helper's hands for more profitable work, but it can also make your job easier. I find the presence of another person distracting, and I prefer to do the layout by myself even when there are others available. When I need to provide an edge to hook my tape to, I nail my speed square in place as I did when laying out floor joists. When I lay out small items, like closets, doors, and windows, I use measuring sticks, which are stiff, lie nice and flat, and don't need to be anchored at one end.

Straightening the Wood

Carpentry textbooks make building a wall seem like a mere matter of assembling parts. On real job sites, though, the sticks of wood that make up a wall are rarely straight and must be persuaded into a reasonably straight line as they're installed. This process usually starts when you're assembling the parts of the wall. In fabricating such things as headers, T-intersections, and corners, you usually have to force the individual pieces of lumber into alignment. If a helper is available, he positions himself at the end of an assembly and steers one piece of lumber flush with an adjoining piece as you work your way up its length, fastening the pieces together. When working alone, though, you can use clamps and wedges in place of that second

Pulling Plywood Decking into Place

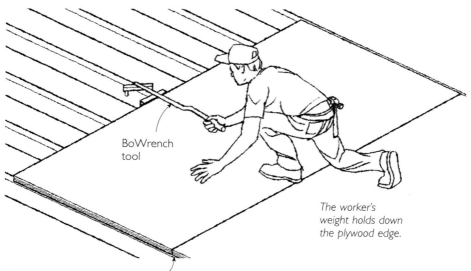

BoWrench tool

The worker's weight holds down the plywood edge.

The tongue of the tongue-and-groove plywood is forced into the groove of the previous row of plywood.

Straightening the Lumber

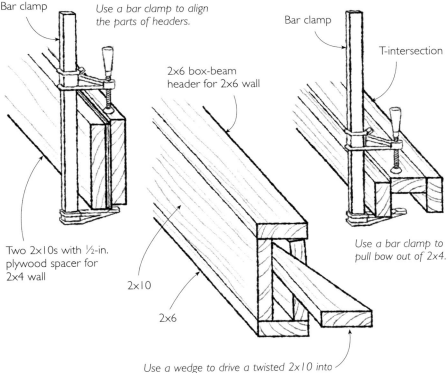

Bar clamp

Use a bar clamp to align
the parts of headers.

Bar clamp

T-intersection

2x6 box-beam
header for 2x6 wall

Two 2x10s with ½-in.
plywood spacer for
2x4 wall

Use a bar clamp to
pull bow out of 2x4.

2x10

2x6

Use a wedge to drive a twisted 2x10 into
alignment with the edge of the top plate.

pair of hands. Some of the techniques that I commonly use are shown in the drawing above. Once the parts are made up and I start building the wall, it's often necessary to torque twisted studs into conformity with the layout lines. Here again, I use my Tweaker tool. After attaching the stud with one nail at the bottom, I crank it into position with the Tweaker as I drive in the top nail.

Erecting Walls

While building walls is a very manageable affair for one person, raising them is a different matter. Walls are large and heavy and, until they are safely braced, can be quite dangerous. There are three different ways to get past the obstacle of raising walls when you're working alone. The first is to call in reinforcements. On many occasions I've scheduled a crew of workers to stop by my job on their way home from other jobs. When they arrive, I have the wall built, squared, sheathed, and ready to tilt into place. We can usually get the wall up and securely braced in about 15 minutes.

Another way to get the wall raised is to build it in manageable sections that you can lift into place yourself. To keep the wall light, I wait to install the sheathing. When the wall is up and secured, I install the sheathing from the outside of the house (see pp. 50-52). I've found that I can usually handle a

10-ft. to 14-ft. section of 2x4 wall or 8 ft. to 12 ft. of 2x6 wall by myself. The size and number of headers in the wall substantially affect the weight and manageability of the wall (the more header material, the harder the wall is to raise).

The third way to raise the wall is to use the proper rigging. Like an auto mechanic who thinks nothing of removing an 800-lb. engine, one carpenter can easily raise an 800-lb. wall—as long as he has the right equipment. A good tool for this job is the Proctor Wall Jack, which is made specifically for raising wood-frame walls. With a pair of these jacks, one person can raise an 8-ft. wall that weighs up to 2,000 lb., which means you can sheathe the wall before you raise it into position. Although I don't own a pair of these jacks, they are high on my wish list of tools.

Whatever method you choose to use, there are two important measures to take before you begin the wall-raising. The first is to provide for some kind of restraint to keep the wall from sliding off the edge of the floor. Some carpenters pin the wall to the layout line with nails driven in at an angle. They usually put these nails through the bottom plate before they square the wall and install the sheathing. As the wall rotates into the upright position, the nails pinning it to the

Beware of the Wind *Because houses are mostly built of large, flat sheets of plywood and other sheathing materials, wind is a serious hazard. It can make walls impossible to control—even for a full crew. And single sheets of plywood, pushed by the wind, can knock a worker off a building or a scaffold. When the wind picks up, respect its force. Avoid working up high on blustery days, particularly with plywood, sheathing, and other sheet materials, and save the wall raising for a calmer tomorrow.*

Using Hoisting Equipment to Raise a Completed Wall

One carpenter can raise a wall weighing up to 2,000 lb. with hoisting equipment such as wall jacks.

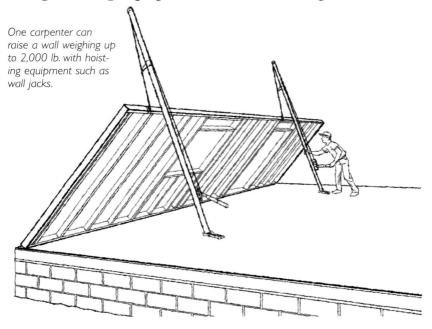

layout line bend. If you raise the wall in unsheathed sections, it's easier to nail scraps vertically to the edge of the floor systems. These scraps project several inches above the top of the floor and keep the wall from sliding off the side.

The second important measure to take before you begin to raise the wall is to provide for some way to brace it securely once it's upright. If you've scheduled a crew to help you raise the wall, this is not really a problem. At least one person holds the wall while others scurry around installing braces. Nor is it a

problem if you're using wall jacks; they support the standing wall as you brace it. If you're working alone and don't have wall jacks, however, you have to make sure you can reach a brace without letting go of the wall (or section of the wall). You can either set a brace where you can reach it after you've raised the wall or, better yet, attach the brace to the floor and prop it up with a temporary brace. (If the wall is unsheathed, you can position the brace between the studs.) Then, when you raise the wall, the brace is ready and all you have to do is nail it to the wall.

Squaring and Sheathing the Walls before Raising

Carpenters usually install the sheathing on exterior walls before they tilt them up. Before they start sheathing the wall, however, they must make sure that the wall is square. (This makes the ends of the wall plumb after it's tilted into position, assuming the foundation is level.) Carpentry crews typically do this by temporarily nailing the bottom plate in position along the layout line and then measuring the diagonals of the framed wall as it lies flat on the floor deck. Someone then taps at the opposite corners until the diagonal measurements become equal and the wall is square.

This trial-and-error procedure works fairly well when two people are doing the measuring, but for a solo carpenter it takes too long. It's easier to use geometry. Create a right triangle using the height of the wall for both sides, then calculate the hypotenuse, which will be the diagonal measurement you use to check for square. As we saw in chapter 2, the formula to find a hypotenuse of a right triangle with two equal sides is:

$$h = \sqrt{2} \times \text{the length of one side}$$

So, for example, the hypotenuse of a 96-in.-high wall would be:

$$h = \sqrt{2} \times 96, \text{ or}$$

$$h = 135\tfrac{3}{4}$$

Once you have the hypotenuse, or diagonal measurement, you can use it to check for square. First, though, you need to "create" the triangle on the wall. You already have one side of the triangle—the end of the frame equal to the height of the wall. To get the other side, measure in along the bottom of the wall the same number of inches as the height of the ceiling and make a mark. In our example, the mark would be at 96 in. (see the drawing on the facing page). Now you have the two sides of your triangle and you can pull the diagonal.

You'll need to hook your tape measure to something to pull the diagonal measurement. You can cut a shallow 45° kerf at the 96-in. mark on the bottom of the wall; or you can scribe a 45° line at the mark, nail a short strip of 1x2 along the line, then hook the tape over the strip. I like this second method better because I don't like to put a kerf in my brand new wall. Insert the hook of your tape measure in the kerf or hook it over the strip, then pull the diagonal measurement.

Squaring Up the Wall

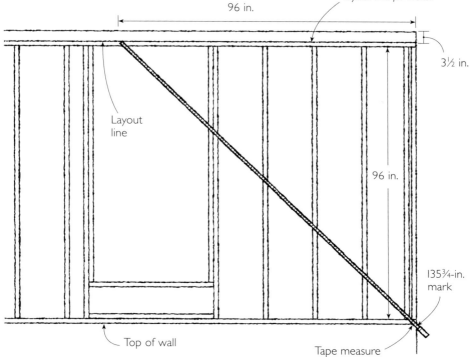

Bottom plate anchors at layout line for walls.

96 in.

3½ in.

Layout line

96 in.

135¾-in. mark

Top of wall

Tape measure

To square up a wall, measure the height and mark that dimension along the bottom plate of the wall. Then pull the diagonal measurement, which can be computed by multiplying the square root of 2 by the height of the wall. The diagonal in this example is 135¾ in. When that dimension intersects with the top corner of the wall, it is square.

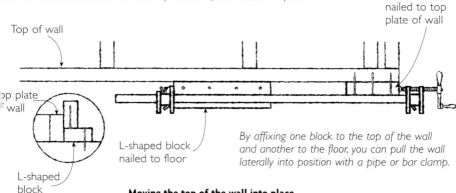

Top of wall

op plate wall

L-shaped block

2x4 block nailed to top plate of wall

L-shaped block nailed to floor

By affixing one block to the top of the wall and another to the floor, you can pull the wall laterally into position with a pipe or bar clamp.

Moving the top of the wall into place

Squaring a Standing Wall

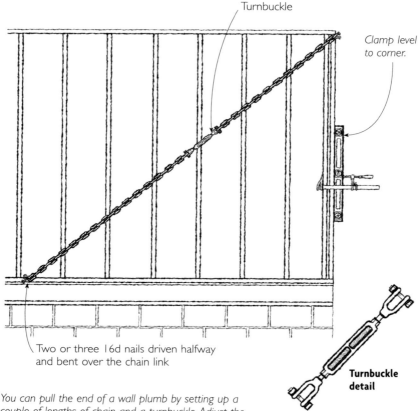

Turnbuckle

Clamp level to corner.

Two or three 16d nails driven halfway and bent over the chain link

Turnbuckle detail

You can pull the end of a wall plumb by setting up a couple of lengths of chain and a turnbuckle. Adjust the turnbuckle until the end of the wall is plumb.

At the same time you're pulling the tape measure, push or pull the wall until the correct diagonal dimension on the tape measure intersects with the top corner. (For the 96-in.-high wall in our example, the wall would be square when the tape measure crossed the top corner at 135¾ in.) This may sound difficult, but the wall is fairly easy to "rack" before it's sheathed. If I have trou-

ble (and I sometimes do), I set up a clamp to hold the tape. To help move the wall into position, I sometimes use a couple of blocks of wood and a bar clamp, as shown in the drawing on p. 47.

As soon as the wall is square, I nail it temporarily to the floor to hold it in that position. Then I install the sheathing on the framed wall.

When I've finished nailing off the sheathing, I remove the nails I installed to hold the wall square. With the sheathing in place, the wall is rigid and square and ready for raising. Once you have the wall up and securely braced, attach it to the floor by nailing through the bottom plate. The wall panel should be square, and consequently the edge of it will be plumb.

Raising the Walls in Unsheathed Sections

There are two advantages to raising a wall without the sheathing. First, it makes it easier to divide the wall into sections; second, it makes each section considerably lighter. But there's a price to pay for these advantages: Without the sheathing the sections of framed wall are not very rigid. These sections have a tendency to sag out of square as they are lifted and installed. So, instead of squaring up each section of the wall as it lies on the floor of the house, it makes sense to postpone the process until after the sections of wall are braced upright and joined together.

Squaring a standing wall

After I get all the sections raised, braced roughly plumb, and nailed securely together, I tie the wall to the house by nailing through the bottom plate into the floor of the house. Next, I check the ends of

the wall with a spirit level to see if they're plumb. (Getting the ends of the wall plumb squares up the wall, as long as the floor is level.) If the wall is racked out-of-square (and it usually is), I clamp my level to the end of the wall. Then I try some old-fashioned pushing and pulling to get it plumb.

If I can't get and hold the corner plumb that way, I set up a turnbuckle with a couple of lengths of chain and pull the end of the wall plumb. I attach the two pieces of chain to the frame of the house, as shown in the drawing on the facing page, then I hook up the turnbuckle. (You can use nails, clamps, or eye-bolts to attach the chains to the wall.) I rotate the turnbuckle with a wrench to draw the ends of the chain together and to pull the top corner of the wall over. I continue rotating the turnbuckle until the level indicates that the end of the wall is perfectly plumb.

When I get the end of the wall plumb, I know the wall is square and I'm ready to install sheathing. You may wonder what I'd have done if I needed to move the top of the wall in the other direction. In that case, I would have set up the turnbuckle and chains at the other end of the wall.

Sheathing a standing wall
I have two different types of brackets for holding up sheathing as I nail it to the outside of the wall. (I typically use ½-in. plywood sheathing and run it horizontally.) To install the first row of sheathing, I use a 64-in.-long steel bracket to hold the sheathing in place. To make the bracket, I had a welder weld a heavy shelf bracket (which I bought at a surplus store for $2) to the bottom 10 in. of a 64-in.-long steel bar. In cross section, the bar is ¼ in. thick and 2 in. wide. The

Installing Plywood Sheathing

To install the first row of plywood sheathing, try using a 64-in.-long bracket.

The bracket supports one side of the sheet while you nail at the other end.

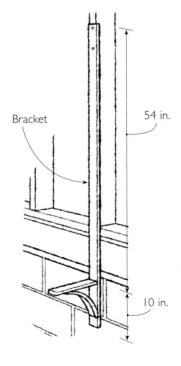

Bracket

54 in.

10 in.

top 54 in. of this bracket is longer than the plywood by 6 in. I nail the bracket to the frame through two holes I drilled in the top 6 in. of the bracket, making sure that the shelf is even with my layout line.

To install the sheathing, I rest one end of the sheet on the bracket as I line up and nail the other end. After driving several nails into the sheathing, I take out the nails that hold up the bracket and it slides to the ground. Because it's quite heavy, I make a real effort to keep the bracket from landing on my foot. Some of the bracket will still be under the sheathing, so I slip it out from behind the sheathing and finish nailing the sheathing to the frame.

For subsequent rows of sheathing, I use a couple of L-shaped plywood brackets, which I call my all-purpose brackets (see the sidebar on p. 89). These are a lot lighter and easier to use than the large steel bracket I used for the first row. I screw the pair of brackets—which are about 14 in. deep—to the wall. Then I set the sheathing on them as I install it (see the drawing below). As I move up the wall, getting the sheathing up on the scaffolding becomes a chal-

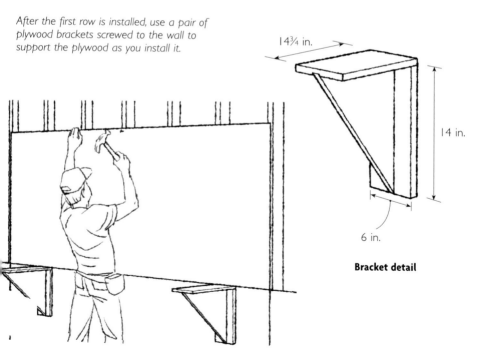

After the first row is installed, use a pair of plywood brackets screwed to the wall to support the plywood as you install it.

14¾ in.

14 in.

6 in.

Bracket detail

Straightening the Wall

2x4 block holds string 1½ in. in from top plate.

Brace nailed to 2x4

2x4 scraps nailed to floor

Bar clamp

Brace

Use level to set corner plumb.

Brace both corners plumb and set the rest of the wall to a string stretched corner to corner. To avoid a false reading caused by contact with the string, set the string 1½ in. away from the top plate.

lenge in its own right. For this job, a C-clamp, affixed to the top edge of the plywood, is just the ticket. Sometimes, I use the C-clamp as a handle to pull the sheet up behind me as I climb the ladder. At other times, I find it easier to use a rope, tied to the C-clamp, to hoist the plywood up to the scaffold.

Plumbing and Straightening the Walls

Because raising a wall is inherently dangerous, carpenters usually secure the wall in an upright posi-

tion as quickly as possible and worry about fine-tuning its position afterward. Hence, the job of plumbing and straightening the wall typically begins with the wall nailed in place at the bottom and braced roughly plumb.

The standard way to adjust the wall is to brace each corner plumb, then set the rest of the wall to a string pulled from corner to corner along the top plate. The first thing I do is remove a brace at one end

Building a Job-Site Sawhorse

Seven years ago, I spent about two hours building a pair of sawhorses using scraps from one of my jobs. I've used the sawhorses almost daily to hold my work at a convenient level for measuring, marking, and cutting and to stand on when work is overhead. For example, I might use a sawhorse when I'm working at ceiling height to straighten a wall. They make my days easier, my work safer—and they're still going strong.

The top of the bench is a 2x6 laid flat. This makes the bench comfortable to sit on and safe to stand on. When I want to secure materials to the bench for cutting, the 2x6 provides a nice flat surface to clamp to. I mortised the side rails ³⁄₈ in. into the legs to make them safe to step on as I climb to the top of the bench; and I installed a sturdy plywood shelf across these side rails to hold tools. I used exterior glue, as well as nails, to make the sawhorses more durable.

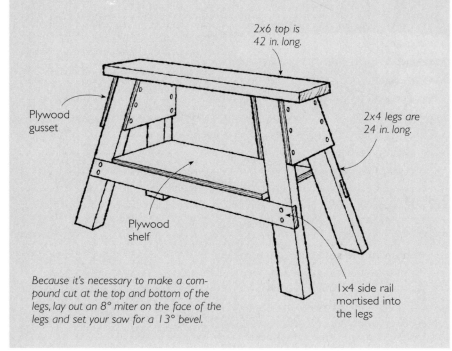

2x6 top is 42 in. long.

Plywood gusset

2x4 legs are 24 in. long.

Plywood shelf

1x4 side rail mortised into the legs

Because it's necessary to make a compound cut at the top and bottom of the legs, lay out an 8° miter on the face of the legs and set your saw for a 13° bevel.

of the wall. Next I clamp a spirit level to the inside of the corner and push or pull the end of the wall until the level indicates that it's plumb. While holding the wall in position, I reattach the brace. After repeating this process at the other end of the wall, I get a wall that has plumb corners but whose intervening length is, in all likelihood, not straight.

To check the wall for straightness, I nail a 2x4 scrap at the top inside edge of each corner, then stretch a string from the face of one block to the other roughly even with the top plate (see the drawing on p. 52). This offsets the string 1½ in. from the plumb corners of the wall. By setting the intervening length of the wall 1½ in. from and parallel to the string I get the wall straight and plumb. To do this I use a 2x4 scrap as a spacer. I remove one or two braces at a time, then nail my spacer block just below the alignment string. Now I push or pull the wall until the edge of the block is even with the string, then reattach the brace. Working systematically down its length, I get the wall arrow straight.

Moving and holding the wall is not as easy as it might seem. Even when extra hands are available, it's often necessary to rig some simple levers to help force the top of the wall into line. The reason for this is not so much the resistance of the wood as its height. The top of the wall is 8 ft. in the air, and it's difficult to apply the needed lateral pressure on something that high. Framing crews use stiff braces to push the wall out and "bow boards" to pull it in. They rely on teamwork: As one person pulls or pushes the wall another quickly nails on a brace. (Not infrequently a third person stays occupied mainly by holding the block in place and telling the others when the wall is in line.)

For a solo builder this technique is physically strenuous, awkward in the best of circumstances, impossible in others. To move and hold the

Pushing and Pulling the Wall into Place

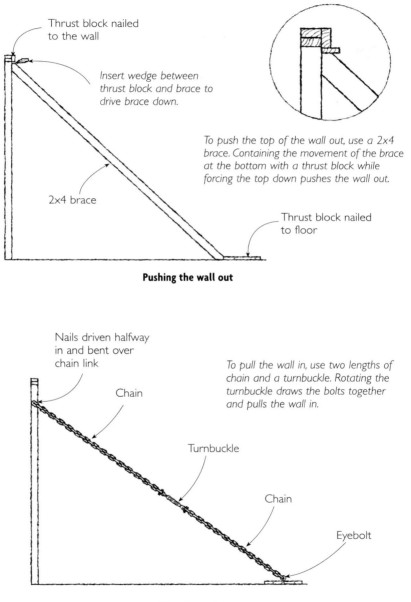

Thrust block nailed to the wall

Insert wedge between thrust block and brace to drive brace down.

To push the top of the wall out, use a 2x4 brace. Containing the movement of the brace at the bottom with a thrust block while forcing the top down pushes the wall out.

2x4 brace

Thrust block nailed to floor

Pushing the wall out

Nails driven halfway in and bent over chain link

To pull the wall in, use two lengths of chain and a turnbuckle. Rotating the turnbuckle draws the bolts together and pulls the wall in.

Chain

Turnbuckle

Chain

Eyebolt

Pulling the wall in

wall precisely in place and, at the same time, install the brace, you need a better rig—one that controls the position of the wall as you adjust it and holds it there as you attach the brace.

Here are the techniques I use. To push the wall out, I set up a 45° brace that's securely anchored at the bottom but not at the top. Driving the brace down exerts a thrusting force that drives the wall out. Although the precise length of the brace is not critical, I usually multiply the height of the wall by 1.414 (the square root of 2) to figure it out. This is the same length as the hypotenuse of my measuring triangle. That means the brace will run at roughly a 45° angle (which isn't essential) and will be long enough to reach the top of the wall. By doing this quick calculation, I ensure that the brace is long enough without having to hold a brace in place and measure how long to cut it to.

This 135¾-in. measurement is the same as the diagonal measurement you used to square the wall. After cutting 1½ in. off the long point of the miter at both the top and bottom, I set the brace in place against the wall. Then I install two "thrust blocks," one on the floor at the bottom of the brace and the other on the wall just above the brace (see the drawing on p. 55). To force the brace down, I simply drive a long wedge between the top of the brace and the thrust block on the wall. This forces the wall out in a gradual and controlled manner.

To pull the wall in, I set up two lengths of chain and a turnbuckle. Rotating the turnbuckle shortens the length of this assembly and thus moves the wall gradually in. I attach the top piece of chain a couple of inches down from the top of the wall and the bottom length of chain about 8 ft. out from the wall. This makes the assembly run at roughly a 45° angle—the exact angle is not important.

On most houses, the roof system is the first structural element that is neither level nor plumb. Roof structures are deliberately pitched to direct rainwater to the outside of the house. When trusses are used for roof framing, the carpentry crew is spared the sometimes-bewildering task of fitting inclined structural members to level and square surfaces. All of this complicated layout, cutting, and fitting is done by the truss manufacturer, and the carpenters need only install these prefabricated components on top of the bearing walls.

On the other hand, when rafters are used, carpenters have to lay out the whole structure and join the individual pieces neatly and securely together. This is more difficult than it might seem. Carpenters not only fit pieces to existing angles, they also create those angles and, in doing so, start from scratch.

If you're working alone, the difficulties posed by the layout are only half the problem. You also have to figure out some way to lift and install the materials that make up the frame. These materials are heavy and unwieldy, and they have to be installed overhead—sometimes far overhead. It's not uncommon, for example, for the ridge of the roof to sit 12 ft. or more off the floor. Yet as difficult as these problems might seem, they can both be overcome. As you'll see, the layout can be simplified by understanding and using the geometry that forms the basis of roof framing and by using a site-built jig. The installation can be managed by developing a well-thought-out plan for lifting the materials into place.

Laying Out the Roof

There are two basic ways to approach the layout of a stick-built roof. The first is to use a nonmathematical approach. The most common nonmathematical technique (and the first one I learned as a young carpenter) is to scribe the rafter in place. To do this, posts are set up to hold the ridge centered at the correct height above the bearing walls. The height of the ridge is determined either by math (I'll discuss the process below) or by scaling the height from the blueprint. Once the ridge is in place, two carpenters (one at each end) hold the rafter material so that it runs past both the ridge and the top plate of the wall. Then they scribe the top and bottom cuts directly onto the rafter material. After the first rafter is cut, it serves as a pattern for the rest of the roof.

If you're working alone, nonmathematical approaches like this one take too much time. It's possible to rig up a bracket to hold the rafter as you mark it, but it's far easier to compute the key dimensions mathematically. This situation is similar to the problems associated with squaring up a foundation, and the math used to solve those problems is also similar to the solution here.

For the balance of this chapter, I'll use an example to walk you through the system I use to lay out and build the most common type of roof, a gable. Some of you may notice that my system differs in several respects from the system that is usually presented in carpentry textbooks. (See the sidebar on p. 60 for a comparison of the two systems.)

Trusses and Rafters

Trusses are structural frames that, all in one, serve the same purpose as rafters and ceiling joists. They are designed by engineers, manufactured by certified fabricators, and shipped to the job. Trusses span long distances and, on most houses, bear only on exterior walls. Because supporting walls usually aren't required on the interior, rooms can be large and open. Trusses offer practical advantages too: They are simple to install, structurally proven, and go up quickly. And because trusses are made from smaller pieces of lumber than rafters and ceiling joists, they can save lumber.

When you consider the advantages of trusses, it's easy to see why they're so popular. Yet trusses are not always the best choice. The structure itself takes up space, which means that part or all of the space between the top chord (at the roofline) and the bottom chord (at the ceiling) is wasted. In a stick-built roof, you can fully exploit the space under the rafters, adding square feet to the living area or attic space. You can also create cathedral ceilings, which can have a dramatic visual impact.

On many jobs, rafters are also easier to use than trusses. Roof trusses require advanced planning, space, a crew, and, occasionally, a crane. If you're building a new house or an addition in an established neighborhood, there might not be enough space for the crane. But even if there is sufficient room to hoist and maneuver trusses, it often makes sense simply to stick-build the whole thing anyway, especially with additions. For a solo builder, of course, the choice is easy: Trusses are almost impossible for one person to install alone.

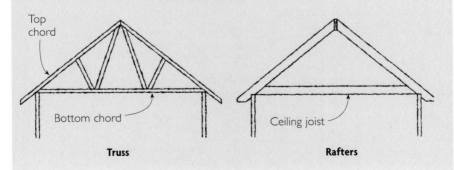

Top chord

Bottom chord

Truss

Ceiling joist

Rafters

Two Paths to the Same Rafter

The main difference between my system of rafter layout and the traditional, or textbook, system is the size of the right triangle used to make the calculations. The traditional way to lay out a rafter is to measure from the outside of one bearing wall to the outside of the other. Divide the measurement in half and you get what's called the "run" of the rafter. It's actually the base of the right triangle used to determine the critical dimensions of the rafters and the height of the ridge.

There are a two things I find confusing about this system. First, it's hard to figure out just where to measure the rafter. The line you have to measure along is somewhere in the middle of the board. The exact location varies with the pitch of the roof, the thickness of the exterior walls, and the size of the rafter material. Second, it's difficult to determine exactly how high up to set the ridge.

In my system (see p. 62), I measure from the inside of one bearing wall to the inside of the other. From this measurement, I subtract the thickness of the ridge. Then I divide the remainder in half to get the base of my measuring triangle, which is different from the base of the right triangle used in the traditional approach. The benefit to this approach is that the rafter measurement is made along the bottom of the rafter, not at some hard-to-determine middle point. To set the ridge at the correct height, I cut a post that's equal to the length of the altitude of the triangle plus the height of the wall.

Traditional Rafter Layout

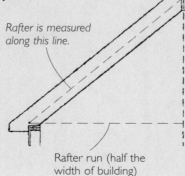

The measuring line in the traditional system of rafter layout extends from the top outside corner of the wall to a point in the center of the ridge.

Rafter is measured along this line.

Rafter run (half the width of building)

Both of these systems are effective ways to calculate the key dimensions of a rafter. If you're already familiar with the "textbook" method, you may wish to continue using it. But, if you're new to rafter layout or if you've had trouble with the textbook method, you may find my system easier to understand. Neither system can be called the right or wrong way because they both result in identical rafters. I simply find my mathematical system easier. If you're working alone, the system you use is not important as long as it enables you to lay out the rafter without having to physically hold it in place.

To show how to take the necessary measurements and do the required calculations to lay out a roof as well as how to build the roof (see pp. 68-76), I'm going to use the example of a gable roof on an addition that is 14 ft. 10 in. (178 in.) wide with a 10-in-12 pitch. To create a cathedral ceiling, a laminated beam 1¾ in. thick by 11⅜ in. wide is specified to serve as a structural ridge. To provide room for insulation, 2x10 rafters are required. Finally, to match the eaves of the house, I need to provide for an overhang on the rafter that ends 12 in. away from the wall of the house.

TRICKS OF THE TRADE

Confused? Draw it Out
If you're having a tough time visualizing the layout, draw it out. Often a simple, free-hand sketch is enough to get things organized in your mind. If you want a neat, scaled drawing, however, you can use the tenths scale on your rafter square. Let each tenth represent an inch, and you'll get a surprisingly accurate drawing— usually within an inch or two of your computations.

Getting Started

It's time to start the roof job in our example, but where do we begin? The first thing to do is measure the inside-to-inside distance between the walls, which have been built out of 2x6s. I clamp a block of wood to the inside of one wall to give me something to hook my tape measure to and take the measurement. The space between the walls is 166 in. This dimension, along with the specified pitch, provides most of the information I need for laying out the roof.

The next step is to subtract the thickness of the ridge from the inside-to-inside dimension, and then divide the remainder by two.

The Geometry of a Common Rafter

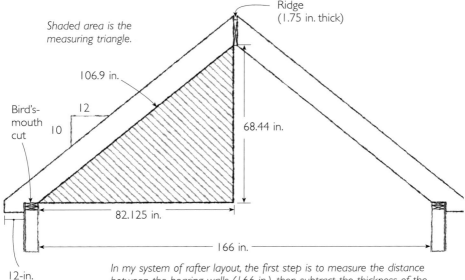

Shaded area is the measuring triangle.

Ridge (1.75 in. thick)

106.9 in.

Bird's-mouth cut

12

10

68.44 in.

82.125 in.

166 in.

12-in. overhang

In my system of rafter layout, the first step is to measure the distance between the bearing walls (166 in.), then subtract the thickness of the ridge (1.75 in.) and divide by 2. This gives me the base of the measuring triangle (82.125 in.).

To establish the altitude of the triangle, which has a 10-in-12 pitch, I divide the base by 12 then multiply by 10 (the result is 68.44). To determine the hypotenuse of the measuring triangle, I use the Pythagorean Theorem (the result is 106.9).

In other words:

166 in. − 1.75 in. = 164.25 in.

164.25 in. ÷ 2 = 82.125 in.

In the traditional parlance of roof framing, this dimension might be called the "run" of the rafter. But that term has come to mean different things to different people. I prefer to use the language of geometry, so I'll call the 82.125-in. dimension the base of my measur-

ing triangle, which is the right triangle highlighted in the drawing above. With this dimension in hand, I can quickly determine the correct height of the ridge and the critical dimensions of the rafter.

Creating the Measuring Triangle
Once the base of the measuring triangle is determined, I need to find the altitude (ridge height) and hypotenuse (rafter dimension) of that triangle. The altitude can't be found by measuring existing condi-

tions the way the base measurement can. Because the altitude doesn't physically exist, I have to create it to satisfy the specifications of the plan. To do this, I apply simple arithmetic to the base dimension. Because I want the measuring triangle to have a 10-in-12 pitch, I know that the altitude has to go up 10 in. for every 12 in. along the base. So I divide the base measurement by 12 to determine exactly how many 12-in. increments there are in the base. Then I multiply the result by 10 to get the altitude of the triangle. Here's how it works for our example:

$$82.125 \text{ (base)} \div 12 = 6.84375$$

$$6.84375 \times 10 = 68.4375$$

So the altitude of the triangle is 68.4375 in., or $68\frac{7}{16}$ in. With the base and altitude measurements in hand, I now calculate the hypotenuse of my measuring triangle using the Pythagorean Theorem.

$$h^2 = a^2 + b^2$$

$$h^2 = 68.4375^2 + 82.125^2$$

$$h^2 = 4683.691 + 6744.516$$

$$h^2 = 11428.21$$

$$h = \sqrt{11428.21}$$

$$h = 106.90 \text{ or } 106\frac{7}{8}$$

As the drawing shows, the altitude and the hypotenuse provide the critical dimensions for this roof frame. The altitude, $68\frac{7}{16}$ in., provides the correct distance above the top plate of the wall to set the bottom of the ridge. The hypotenuse, $106\frac{7}{8}$ in., provides the correct distance to measure between the top and bottom cuts of the rafter. As the drawing shows, this measurement is taken along the bottom edge of the rafter.

Laying Out and Cutting the Rafters

Although it's not essential, I begin this part of the job by fabricating a rafter jig. I have several different manufactured squares that I can use to lay out the angled cuts of the rafter, but I prefer to use this jig. You probably wonder why I go to the trouble of making this jig when I already have several store-bought tools that serve the same purpose. There are four reasons.

First, I find it easier to visualize the cuts with the jig than with any manufactured tool. Second, I find the jig very effective for making fast, repetitive layouts. Third, I use the plumb edge of the jig as a cutting guide for my circular saw. And finally, I use the jig again and again later on, while I'm framing the gable, finishing the eaves and rake, or marking any material that follows the pitch of the roof. I've never invested time in making a

A 10-in-12 Rafter Jig

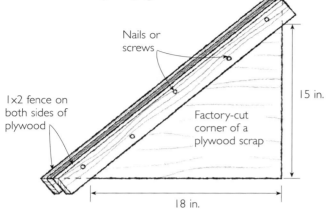

Nails or screws

1x2 fence on both sides of plywood

Factory-cut corner of a plywood scrap

15 in.

18 in.

rafter jig that wasn't returned many times over by the end of the job. And, when I'm done, I save the jig for future jobs that call for the same pitch.

To make the jig, I attach a fence at a 10-in-12 pitch across the corner of a piece of plywood. This piece must be square, so I look for a scrap that came off the end of a sheet of plywood and thus has a factory-cut corner. For use with 2x6 rafter material, I'd lay out this jig by measuring and marking 10 in. up from the corner and 12 in. out. Connecting those points with a fence completes the jig. But a jig that size is not large enough for the 2x10 rafters in our example.

To expand the jig to fit larger rafters without changing the pitch, I multiply the altitude and the base

by the same number—1.5. I end up with a jig that has an altitude of 15 in. and a base of 18 in., but the same 10-in-12 pitch. I mark these measurements on the plywood, then connect the two marks with a straight line. I draw a second line parallel to and about 2 in. above the first. I cut along this second line, and the 2-in. space between the two lines provides a surface to which I attach a 1x2 fence, placing it carefully along the hypotenuse of the layout.

Although not necessary, I generally attach a fence on both sides of the plywood because the jig comes in handy after the roof frame is completed, and having the fence on both sides of the jig allows me to reverse the jig for these other jobs. To use the jig, I hold the fence against the top edge of the rafter

Laying Out a Rafter

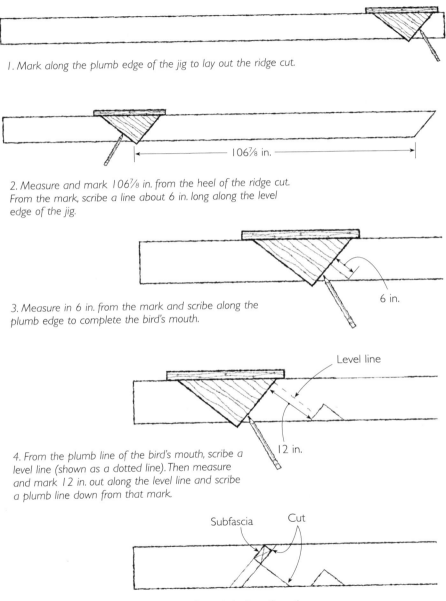

1. Mark along the plumb edge of the jig to lay out the ridge cut.

2. Measure and mark 106⅞ in. from the heel of the ridge cut. From the mark, scribe a line about 6 in. long along the level edge of the jig.

— 106⅞ in. —

3. Measure in 6 in. from the mark and scribe along the plumb edge to complete the bird's mouth.

6 in.

Level line

4. From the plumb line of the bird's mouth, scribe a level line (shown as a dotted line). Then measure and mark 12 in. out along the level line and scribe a plumb line down from that mark.

12 in.

Subfascia   Cut

5. Use the jig to draw in the subfascia. Extend the lines from the inside and bottom of the subfascia to finish the rafter-tail layout.

stock and scribe along the vertical (15-in.) side for plumb cuts and along the horizontal (18-in.) side for level cuts. Keep in mind that throughout this whole layout process the rafter jig is oriented the same way—with the fence held snugly against the top edge of the rafter and the plumb edge to the ridge end of the rafter.

Now comes the fun part. With the critical dimensions and the rafter jig in hand, the rest of the job is a stroll in the park. The first thing I do is scribe along the plumb edge of the jig to mark the ridge cut (Step 1 in the drawing on p. 65). After I make the ridge cut, I mea-

sure the 106⅞-in. dimension (the hypotenuse) from the heel of the cut along the bottom of the rafter (Step 2). To make this measurement, I clamp a square across the rafter to provide something to hook my tape measure to. After marking the rafter at 106⅞ in., I slide the rafter jig to the mark and scribe the level cut line. Because the wall is 6 in. thick, I measure in 6 in. along the level line and mark. Then I slide the jig to this mark and scribe down along the plumb edge to finish off the bird's-mouth layout (Step 3).

With the main part of the rafter layout complete, it's time to work on the rafter tail. First, use the jig to scribe a level line out from the plumb line of the bird's mouth. I usually use a dotted line here to distinguish this line from the others. Because the plumb line of the bird's mouth is even with the outside of the wall, all I have to do in this case is measure 12 in. out along the dotted line to establish where the end of the eaves (or overhang) should be (Step 4). After marking this point, I slide the jig into place and mark along the plumb edge. But I won't be cutting along that line. I generally install a 2x4 subfascia when I frame the eaves, so I draw the subfascia full-sized inside the line I've just marked (Step 5). The sketched-in 2x4 not only shows me where to make my plumb cut on the rafter tail (1½ in. in from the 12-in. mark to accommodate the subfascia); it also shows me where to make the level cut. As the drawing on p. 65 shows, I scribe a level line even with the bottom of the 2x4 to complete the rafter-tail layout.

Carpenters often cut the first rafter they lay out, then use it as a pattern to lay out the rest of the rafters. Lining up and holding this pattern rafter is awkward for one person, though, so I use a different technique—I make a measuring stick. After I lay out the first rafter, I hold a strip of wood against the rafter and transfer the points where the four lines at the tail of the rafter intersect with the bottom edge of the board. I use this custom measuring stick to lay out the tail section of each succeeding rafter. After making the ridge cut and pulling the 106⅞-in. measurement, I align the first mark on my measuring stick with the 106⅞-in.

Using a Measuring Stick to Transfer the Layout

After laying out the first rafter, mark on a strip of wood the four points where the bird's mouth and rafter-tail layout lines intersect with the bottom of the rafter. Now you can use this measuring stick to transfer the layout to subsequent rafters.

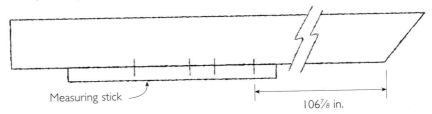

Measuring stick

106⅞ in.

1. After marking the 106⅞-in. measurement, align the measuring stick and transfer the other three marks.

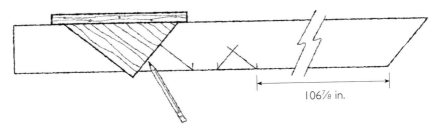

106⅞ in.

2. Use the rafter jig to extend the layout from the marks.

Reference Mark on Rafter Measuring Stick *To avoid the possibility of lining up your measuring stick backwards, put a circle or other distinguishing symbol on the first mark on the stick.*

mark and transfer the other three marks to the rafter. Now I slide the rafter jig in place and extend lines out from these marks to lay out the tail of the rafter.

Building the Roof

In the section on creating the measuring triangle (pp. 62-63), I found the two critical dimensions for this roof frame. You've just seen how I used one of the critical dimensions, the hypotenuse, to lay out the rafter. In this section, I'll describe how I use the other critical dimension, the altitude, to set the ridge to the proper height. After I describe how I install the ridge, I'll show how I cut the ridge to length and then lay out the points where the rafters engage the ridge. Finally, I'll explain how I install the rafters and the plywood roof deck.

Setting the Ridge
The first step in setting the ridge is to make a couple of posts to support it at the correct height.

Because the walls in this addition are 97½ in. high, the posts need to be 97½ in. + 68⁷⁄₁₆ in. (the roof altitude), or 165¹⁵⁄₁₆ in. high. To make each post, I cut two 2x4s this length, then nail them to a 2x4 that is about 8 in. longer. This third 2x4 stiffens the post and serves as a "saddle," or niche, to hold the ridge on top of the posts.

I center the posts between the bearing walls and brace them plumb in both directions. I typically place each post about 18 in. in from the end of the floor system. Because I need to leave one side of the post open for raising the ridge, I place all the braces that run perpendicular to the bearing walls on the same side of the posts. When I install these braces, I don't worry about bracing the top third of the posts; in fact, I like to leave some play. When I install the rafters, which will all be cut to the same dimension, they'll center the ridge. The primary concern at this stage is getting the ridge at the right height.

A ridge as large as the one specified in this plan is quite heavy. To get it on top of the posts, I have to lift one end at a time and work it up the post in manageable increments (see the drawing on the facing page). To hold the ridge as I step it up the posts, I use the same all-purpose L-shaped brackets I

Raising the Ridge

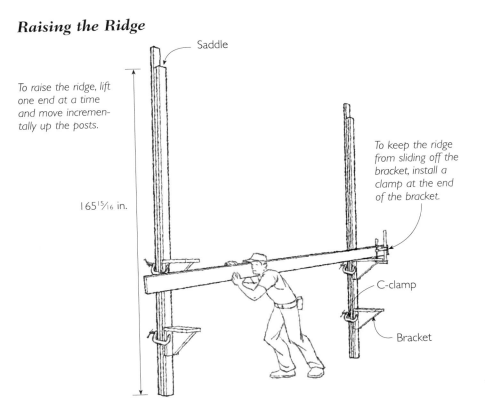

Saddle

To raise the ridge, lift one end at a time and move incrementally up the posts.

165¹⁵⁄₁₆ in.

To keep the ridge from sliding off the bracket, install a clamp at the end of the bracket.

C-clamp

Bracket

used for sheathing the outside of the walls. I begin by clamping a bracket on each post about 3 ft. off the floor. Because of the weight of the ridge, I use two C-clamps for each bracket. I lift one end, then the other to set the ridge on this pair of brackets.

I keep my hand on the ridge beam throughout this process, but once it's in place on the brackets, I clamp it to one of the posts with a one-hand bar clamp. (I set this clamp within reach before I pick

up the ridge.) I can now let go of the beam and set up a second pair of brackets about 3 ft. above the first. After moving the ridge to this level, I take off the first pair of brackets and set them above the second. I repeat this process, leapfrogging my brackets upward as I go, until I have the ridge securely set in the saddle atop the posts.

Good scaffolding is a vital part of roof-building. As soon as I get the ridge about 6 ft. off the floor, I set up a section of pipe scaffolding, which provides a secure surface to stand on as I move the ridge up another 6 ft. or so. After moving the ridge another 5 ft. or 6 ft., I set up a second row of scaffolding on top of the first. When I finish setting the ridge, my scaffolding is in place for building the rest of the roof. I want to re-emphasize here how important it is to control this heavy, potentially dangerous beam at every point of this process. If you decide to use this technique, please take precautions (see the safety tip above).

Cutting the Ridge and Laying Out Rafter Locations

When I clamp the ridge to the saddle on top of the posts I leave it running long, with the intention of cutting it in place. I have to cut the ridge directly above the outside edge of the floor system. To see why I need to do this and how I go about getting this cut in the right spot, think about this addition in plan view. If you look at the drawing on the facing page, you can see that the ridge extends 1 ft. or so beyond the edge of the floor system. Notice that the edge of the floor system runs from the end of one bearing wall to the end of the other. Because the foundation has been carefully squared up, the floor system that rests on it is a true rectangle. Thus, the edge of the floor system runs perpendicular to the bearing walls.

To get the end of the ridge in line with the ends of the bearing walls, then, I have to cut it at a point that's directly above the outside edge of the floor system. Once I have the ridge cut at this point, I pull identical layouts from the ends of both bearing walls and the end of ridge. Then, when I install rafters on these layout marks, they run perpendicular to the bearing walls and the ridge. In essence, I'm transferring the square shape of the floor system up to the roof frame.

Getting the Roof Frame Square

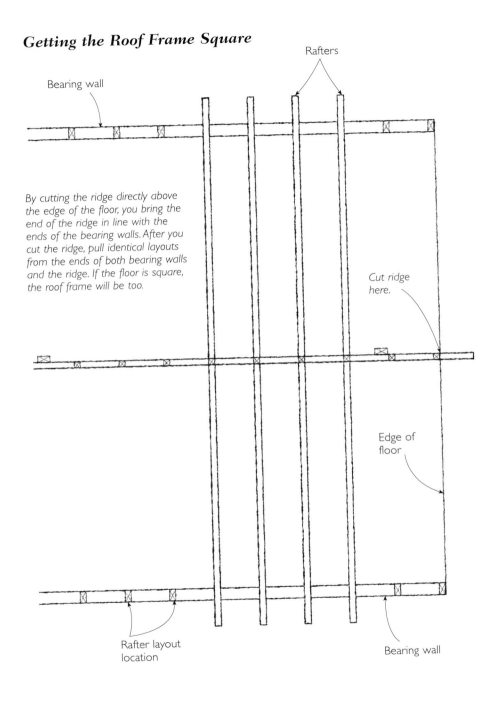

Rafters

Bearing wall

By cutting the ridge directly above the edge of the floor, you bring the end of the ridge in line with the ends of the bearing walls. After you cut the ridge, pull identical layouts from the ends of both bearing walls and the ridge. If the floor is square, the roof frame will be too.

Cut ridge here.

Edge of floor

Rafter layout location

Bearing wall

Cutting the Ridge Even with the Outside Edge of the Floor

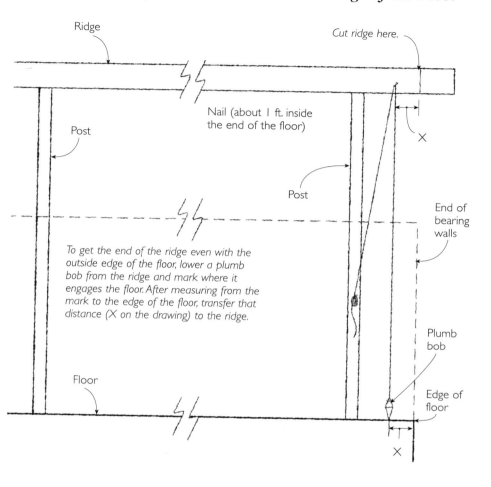

Ridge

Cut ridge here.

Nail (about 1 ft. inside the end of the floor)

Post

Post

X

End of bearing walls

To get the end of the ridge even with the outside edge of the floor, lower a plumb bob from the ridge and mark where it engages the floor. After measuring from the mark to the edge of the floor, transfer that distance (X on the drawing) to the ridge.

Plumb bob

Floor

Edge of floor

X

That's why I cut the ridge directly above the outside edge of the floor system; here's how I do it. First I drive a nail in the side of the ridge positioned (by eye) about 10 in. inside the edge of the floor. I angle this nail down as I hammer it halfway in. Then I loop the string

of my plumb bob over the nail, lower the bob, and mark where it engages the floor. I measure the distance from the mark to the edge of the floor, then climb the scaffold and measure the same amount out from the nail to establish the point that is precisely plumb to the out-

Using a Plumb Bob

Here are a few simple tricks I've discovered that make using a plumb bob easy.

• Use a good, heavy bob (24 oz.) and braided nylon mason's line. Braided line is better than twisted line because it doesn't unwind and stretch from the weight of the bob.

• Set up a simple rig to hold the string as you lower the bob. To lower a bob from the side of an overhead structure, drive a nail in at an angle and loop the string over the nail. To lower a bob from the underside of an overhead structure, install a small

eyebolt and thread the string through the eye.

• Rig up a cleat to tie off the string once the bob is lowered into position. You can buy a small cleat at any hardware store, but I find it more convenient to fashion one out of two nails.

• To bring the bob quickly to a standstill, rest a square or a block of wood on the floor. With this method you can hold the block or square steady and it contacts the bob only at its widest point (and thus does not jar it out of alignment).

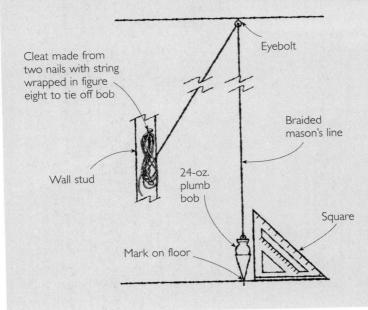

Cleat made from two nails with string wrapped in figure eight to tie off bob

Eyebolt

Braided mason's line

Wall stud

24-oz. plumb bob

Mark on floor

Square

Installing the Rafters

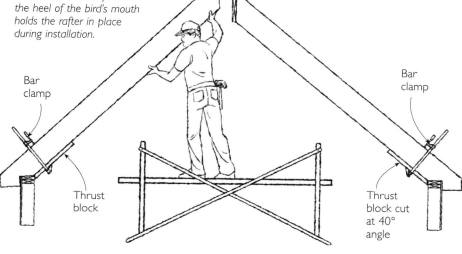

A thrust block clamped at the heel of the bird's mouth holds the rafter in place during installation.

Ridge

Bar clamp

Bar clamp

Thrust block

Thrust block cut at 40° angle

Converting Pitch to Degrees

To convert the plumb-cut layout of a 10-in-12 pitch into degrees, place a Speed Square on the edge of a board and rotate it on the pivot until the 10-in-12 pitch (in the common-rafter scale) is even with the edge of the board. Then look at the degree scale; it should read just less than 40° in. To use a Quick Square, adjust the fence to the 10-pitch mark and read the corresponding degrees in the degree scale.

side edge of the floor. (For more information on how to use a plumb bob see the sidebar on p. 73.) Using a square, I draw a straight line through this mark and cut to the line. The end of the ridge is now even with the ends of the bearing walls, and now all I have to do is pull identical layouts from all three ends.

Installing the Rafters

Holding and installing the rafters on an addition like this is a surprisingly easy job. To keep the rafter from sliding off the wall as I install it at the ridge, I clamp a 2x2 thrust block at the heel of the bird's-

Installing the Subfascia

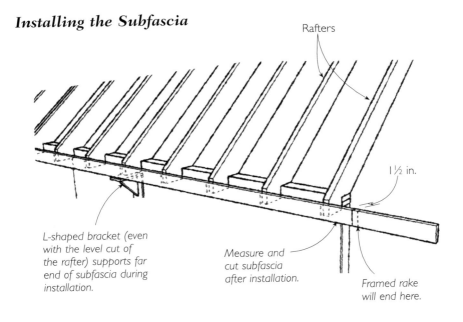

Rafters

1½ in.

L-shaped bracket (even with the level cut of the rafter) supports far end of subfascia during installation.

Measure and cut subfascia after installation.

Framed rake will end here.

mouth cut (see the drawing on the facing page). I cut this block at an angle so it fully and accurately engages the top of the wall. The angle of this cut is the same as the plumb cut of the rafter, and it can be laid out with the rafter jig. It's faster to zip through this cut with a miter saw, so I set my saw to a 40° miter and slice off the angle without even making a line. (To convert from angles described in pitch to angles described in degrees see the box on the facing page.)

After clamping the thrust block to the rafter, I pull the rafter up on the scaffold and, holding the upper end above the ridge, slide the lower end of it toward the wall. When the thrust block engages the wall, I lower the upper end of the rafter down against the ridge. In that position it's wedged in place and, if I want, I can take a coffee break before nailing it off.

Installing the Plywood Deck

After installing the rafters, I turn my attention to the plywood deck. I begin this process by setting up pipe scaffolding under the eaves of the roof. Once the scaffolding is set up, I install the 2x4 subfascia on the ends of the rafter tails (see the drawing above). To support the

Laying Down the Plywood

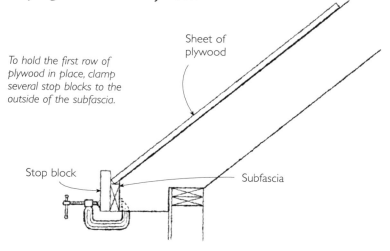

To hold the first row of plywood in place, clamp several stop blocks to the outside of the subfascia.

Sheet of plywood

Stop block

Subfascia

far end of the board, I screw an L-shaped bracket to the wall, with the shelf of the bracket flush with the level cut of the rafter tail. (For more on the L-shaped bracket, see the sidebar on p. 89.) I install the subfascia long, measure and mark it in place, and then cut if off with my circular saw. It's easier to make this cut before installing the roof deck. Also, it's important to make the cut 1½ in. short of the desired width of the framed rake so the next long board—the barge rafter—can run past the subfascia.

I then clamp several scraps of 2x4 to the outside face of the subfascia, making sure the scraps project a few inches above the tops of the rafters. These scraps act as stop blocks for the plywood. Next I fetch a sheet of plywood. To get the plywood up to the roof, I use a C-clamp as a handle and pull the sheet up after me as I climb the ladder. Once I have it at the roof, I flop it into place across the rafters 1 ft. or so above the projecting blocks. I can now slide the plywood accurately into place against the stop blocks.

After installing the first row of plywood, I install roof jacks and work off them as I set the subsequent rows of plywood. To push or pull the rafters into conformity with the layout, I use bar clamps and spreaders, just as I did when I installed the floor deck.

When you finish framing the roof of a house or addition, you have reached a watershed in the job. This is especially true for solo builders. The structural phase of the job is now a thing of the past, and you no longer have to envision and lay out new elements or lift and install the brawny materials that hold up the building. From this point on, you'll be finishing the space you've already built. The materials will be noticeably lighter, and, for the most part, the layout chores will be simpler and easier. But this does not mean that you're suddenly home free—a new set of challenges emerges just as the previous ones are disposed of.

Because you're now working with an existing structure, you have to contend with the imperfections of that structure. To fit materials to a frame that is inevitably flawed, you'll measure the standing structure frequently. A large proportion of these measurements are along walls and other vertical surfaces, but for the first time you'll have to measure and install materials to the underside of horizontal surfaces, such as ceilings and eaves.

However, you can no longer routinely clamp, nail, or screw brackets and jigs to the work surface. Closing the walls and ceilings covers most of the suitable clamping surfaces, and because the new sur-faces are final and open to view, putting nail or screw holes in them is not always acceptable.

At this stage, there are typically several nonstructural details that need to be finished off. Among these are partitions and gable-end walls, roof overhangs (eaves and rakes), windows and doors, roof shingles, and siding. All of these tasks can be done working alone. In this chapter, I'll present these tasks in the order that I typically do them. It's important to take note of the sequence that I work in because these techniques have to be done in the proper order to work well.

Framing Nonbearing Walls

When building nonbearing partitions and gable-end walls, carpentry crews usually start by laying out the bottom plate at the floor, and then transfer the layout up to the ceiling using a spirit level and a straightedge. If you're working alone, this technique is difficult because it requires you to do three different things that are spread from the floor to the ceiling. After clamping a level to a straight 2x4, you first have to hold this assembly precisely on the layout line on the bottom plate, then swing it until the level reads plumb, and, at the same time, mark the underside of the ceiling (or the top plate of the wall).

It's possible for one person to do this, but I find it a lot easier to use a plumb bob. There's one odd thing about using a plumb bob, though: It works best when you start at the top and work down. So when I build any wall, I install the top plate first and then transfer the layout down with my plumb bob.

Straight Walls

To determine the layout for a straight wall, I must first find out how far the partition needs to be from the nearest standing wall. Then I measure and mark that dimension on a strip of wood. I use this measuring stick to lay out the location of the plate on the ceiling. Before I lift the top plate into place, I nail a 2x4 scrap on the wall

Laying Out and Installing the Top Plate

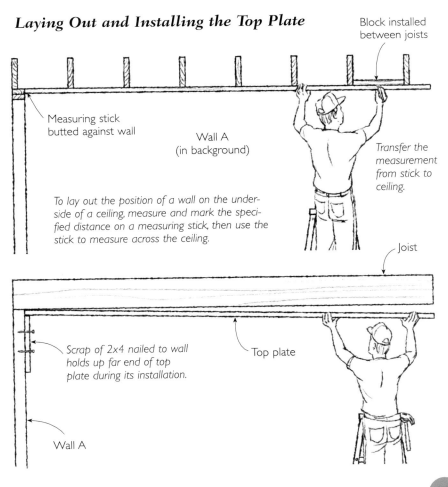

Block installed between joists

Measuring stick butted against wall

Wall A (in background)

Transfer the measurement from stick to ceiling.

To lay out the position of a wall on the underside of a ceiling, measure and mark the specified distance on a measuring stick, then use the stick to measure across the ceiling.

Joist

Scrap of 2x4 nailed to wall holds up far end of top plate during its installation.

Top plate

Wall A

Transferring the Location of the Top Plate to the Floor

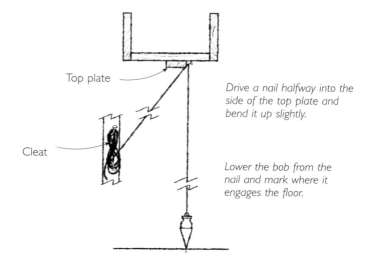

Top plate

Cleat

Drive a nail halfway into the side of the top plate and bend it up slightly.

Lower the bob from the nail and mark where it engages the floor.

a little more than 1½ in. down from the ceiling. This block supports one end of the top plate while I nail the other. If I think ahead, I mark the layout on the top plate before I install it; if not, I use a measuring stick to mark the stud locations on the installed plate.

The next step is to lower the plumb bob from the side of the top plate to mark the location of the bottom plate (see the drawing above). Then, after nailing off the bottom plate, I return to the top plate, drive nails in at each stud location, and use the plumb bob to transfer the layout down to the bottom plate. After marking the plate, I cut and install the studs.

Walls that Follow the Roofline

When the top plate follows the underside of the roof—as it would on a partition beneath a cathedral ceiling or on a gable-end wall—the layout is a little more difficult. To get the studs on the normal 16-in. layout, I determine the hypotenuse of a right triangle that's the same angle as the roof and has a 16-in. base. It's easy to determine this dimension mathematically, using the same procedure I used when I created the measuring triangle for the roof frame. But for small layouts like this, I generally use my rafter square to make a full-sized drawing. It's fast, foolproof, simple to do because it doesn't require calculations, and easier to visualize.

Laying Out an Angled Top Plate

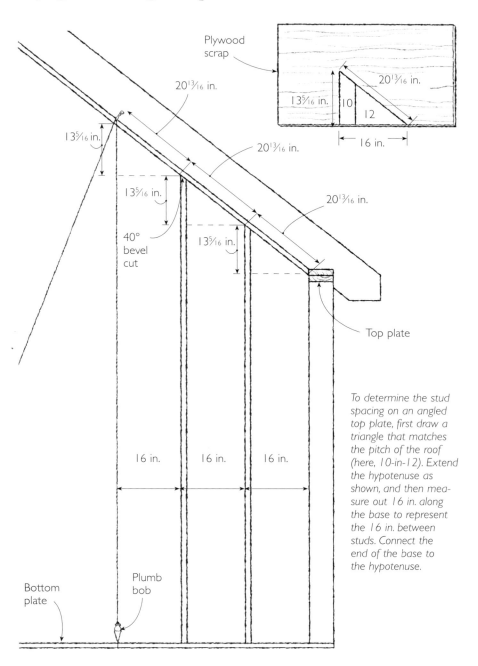

Plywood scrap

20¹³⁄₁₆ in.

13⁵⁄₁₆ in.

10

12

16 in.

20¹³⁄₁₆ in.

20¹³⁄₁₆ in.

13⁵⁄₁₆ in.

13⁵⁄₁₆ in.

20¹³⁄₁₆ in.

13⁵⁄₁₆ in.

40° bevel cut

Top plate

16 in.

16 in.

16 in.

Plumb bob

Bottom plate

To determine the stud spacing on an angled top plate, first draw a triangle that matches the pitch of the roof (here, 10-in-12). Extend the hypotenuse as shown, and then measure out 16 in. along the base to represent the 16 in. between studs. Connect the end of the base to the hypotenuse.

I begin the layout by drawing a right triangle that matches the pitch of the roof—in this case 10-in-12, so the sides are 10 in. and 12 in. (see the drawing on p. 81). When I finish this triangle, I extend the hypotenuse several inches beyond the triangle and extend the base to 16 in. The new baseline is the correct length for measuring between studs. I draw a line perpendicular to the base connecting the 16-in. mark on the base to the hypotenuse to finish the measuring triangle. I measure the hypotenuse, which is $20^{13}/_{16}$ in. for a 10-in-12 pitch. This measurement tells me the increments I need to lay out on the top plate to end up with studs spaced 16 in. apart.

The final step is to measure, cut, and install the studs. Once again,

I use the right triangle I created for layout. Looking at the altitude of the right triangle, I can see that each stud will be $13^{5}/_{16}$ in. longer (as you approach the peak) than its immediate predecessor in the layout. Instead of carefully measuring every stud, I cut the first stud a few inches long, then add $13^{5}/_{16}$ in. to each succeeding stud. Now I hold each rough-cut stud in place on the layout lines and scribe the top cut. After setting my miter saw to a 40° bevel (the equivalent of a 10-in-12 pitch), I cut along the scribed line, then install the stud. Notice that I've completely violated the old adage "measure twice, cut once." Once a miter saw is set up, cutting is faster than measuring; and marking a piece directly is more accurate than measuring a distance, then transferring that measurement to the piece.

TRICKS OF THE TRADE

Scaffolding Setup
The same scaffolding setup can often be used for several phases of the job. On my last large addition, I set up scaffolding after I completed the roof frame and used it to sheathe the exterior of the house, frame and trim the roof overhangs, set the windows, and run the siding. Then I left it in place for the painter.

Finishing the Eaves and Rakes

Carpentry crews often manage to get through the job of finishing the roof overhangs by working off ladders, but good scaffolding is just about essential for a solo builder (see pp. 33-35). When you set up the scaffolding, keep in mind that the most intricate work is at the corners, where the eaves meet the rakes, so it's important to get the scaffolding set up so that you can move easily around a corner. Another consideration is to get the scaffolding at the right height. Framing and trimming the overhangs might take several days, so take the time to set things up at a comfortable working height. You don't want to be reaching or stooping. I've found that putting the scaffold 60 in. below the undersides of the eaves and rakes works well for me (I'm 5 ft. 7 in. tall).

Once the scaffolding is in place, you face a familiar pair of problems. First, how do you measure the long pieces that make up the eaves and rakes? Second, how do you hold up the far end of these pieces as you install them? The first problem is not as difficult as it might seem. I avoid a lot of the measurements involved in this job by installing the pieces long and then cutting them in place. Where cutting in place is not practical, I temporarily attach the piece and mark it directly rather than taking and transferring a measurement. The second problem is also fairly easy to solve. I use a number of simple, site-built brackets—held in place with screws, nails, or clamps—to support the far end of the boards.

Technically, the first step in this job is installing the subfascia (also called the rough fascia), but I do that before I install the roof deck. For more on installing the subfascia, see pp. 75-76.

TRICKS OF THE TRADE

Using a Modified Chalk Box
I often clamp my modified chalk-box assembly in place, but sometimes it's better to nail or screw it in place. When I use fasteners, I offset the nails or screws from the chalkline, which allows me to attach the line block without puncturing the finished surface of the siding.

The Barge Rafter

Before I install the barge rafter, which forms the outside edge of the overhanging rake, I snap a chalkline on the underside of the overhanging plywood. This line represents the inside of the barge rafter. In most cases, I drive a nail halfway in to hold one end of the string as I snap lines. Driving a nail into the underside of this unanchored and springy plywood overhang would be difficult, and, in any event, the line would have a tendency to fall off the nail.

Instead of using a nail, I use a chalk box that has the end of the line secured to a block of wood (see the drawing on p. 96). Using a one-hand C-clamp, it's easy to clamp the line-block assembly in place to the underside of the plywood and snap the line overhead.

Building the Rake

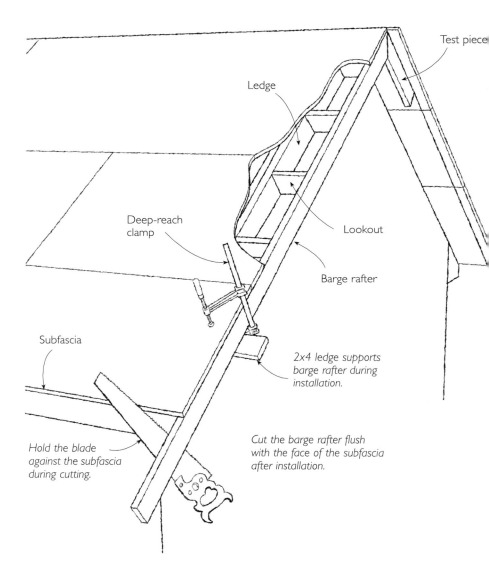

Test piece

Ledge

Deep-reach clamp

Lookout

Barge rafter

Subfascia

2x4 ledge supports barge rafter during installation.

Hold the blade against the subfascia during cutting.

Cut the barge rafter flush with the face of the subfascia after installation.

After I snap this line for the barge rafter, I install a 2x4 ledge under the roof deck and against the house. Next I install a series of 2x4 blocks (sometimes called lookouts) that run out from the ledge and end at the chalkline. The barge rafter and plywood soffit are nailed to the lookouts. I use a 5-in.-deep bar clamp to hold the lookouts in place as I nail through the roof deck to attach them. I also toenail them into the ledge.

Next, I cut and install the barge rafter. I begin this process by cutting the top of the barge rafter to the proper miter (40° for a 10-in-12 roof). To support the bottom end of this board, I use my 5-in.-deep bar clamp to hold a 2x4 scrap on the underside of one of the lookouts. The scrap extends a few inches past the end of the lookout and serves as a temporary shelf. In addition to supporting the weight of the barge rafter, this shelf allows me to move the rafter forward or backward as I adjust its position.

To help get the barge rafter in the right position, I use a test piece cut at the proper miter (40° in this example) to represent the opposing barge rafter. As soon as I'm satisfied with the fit at the converging angles of the overhang, I nail the barge rafter in place. After securing the barge rafter, I use a sharp handsaw to cut it flush with the face of the subfascia. To get a good square cut, I hold the side of the sawblade against the subfascia with one hand, while I saw with the other.

Notice that I did not try to measure the distance and fit both ends at the same time. Whenever possible, I leave one end long and carefully fit the other end. Only after I'm satisfied with the fit at the first end, do I concern myself with the second end—where I either cut or mark the piece in place.

Eave Frames

Finishing off the frame of the eaves is straightforward. After leveling in from the subfascia and snapping a chalkline, I nail a 2x4 ledge at the line. To support the far end of the ledge, I go around to the gable side of the house and nail a 2x4 that extends several inches beyond the corner (see the drawing on p. 86). This projecting board holds up one end of the ledge as I nail it in place. I leave the ledge long, then plumb down from the barge rafter, mark, and cut the ledge in place with my circular saw. The portion that projects out beyond the gable-end wall becomes an integral part of the rake return.

Framing the rest of the eaves and rake return are jobs that don't require difficult measurements or long boards. But using clamps makes these tasks go more smoothly for a

Installing the Ledge

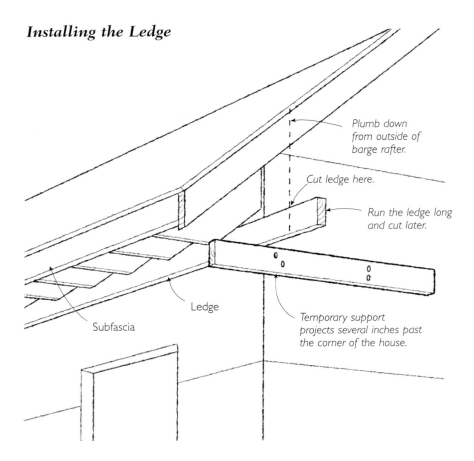

Plumb down from outside of barge rafter.

Cut ledge here.

Run the ledge long and cut later.

Ledge

Subfascia

Temporary support projects several inches past the corner of the house.

solo builder. Typically, I install a series of 2x4 cross-blocks running across the eaves from the subfascia to the ledge. As I install each cross-block, I use a one-hand bar clamp to hold a scrap of wood to the underside of the ledge. The scrap acts as a little shelf, holding up the inside of the cross-block while I nail through the subfascia and into the other end. I also use clamps to hold materials in place as I frame the rake return.

Finish Materials

As soon as I've framed the eaves and rakes, I fasten the finish materials to them. I use the same basic methods to install the finish materials as I used on the underlying frame. First, I install the fascia running long. To hold it in place, I clamp a bracket to one of the cross-blocks (see the drawing on p. 88). Because the bottom of the fascia has to be about $1\frac{7}{8}$ in. below the bottom of the subfascia, I make

Installing Cross-Block in Eaves

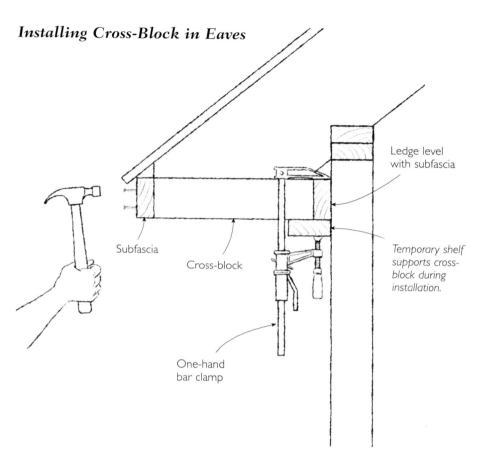

Ledge level with subfascia

Subfascia

Cross-block

Temporary shelf supports cross-block during installation.

One-hand bar clamp

this bracket roughly L-shaped. After nailing off the fascia, I cut it in place with my handsaw, holding the blade flat against the barge rafter as I saw. Then I install the rake board. To hold up the lower end of the board, I clamp an L-shaped bracket to the underside of one of the lookouts. For this clamping chore, I use a deep-reaching bar clamp, with one pressure point under the bracket and the other on top of the roof deck.

As I did with the barge rafter, I let the bottom of the rake board run long while I fuss with the fit at the apex of the overhang. When I get a satisfactory fit, I nail the rake in place and use my handsaw to cut the bottom flush with the face of the fascia. Cutting and fitting the final pieces of the rake return presents no special difficulties for a solo carpenter.

Attaching the Fascia

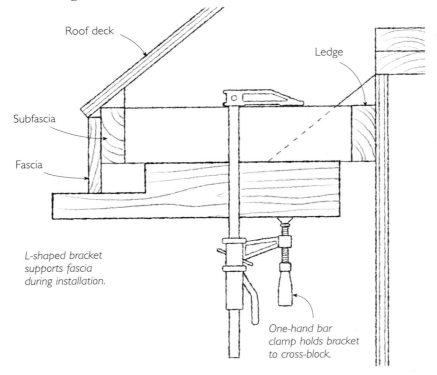

Roof deck

Ledge

Subfascia

Fascia

*L-shaped bracket
supports fascia
during installation.*

*One-hand bar
clamp holds bracket
to cross-block.*

The Soffit

The final phase of the job is to
install the plywood soffit that goes
on the underside of the eaves and
the rakes. To make the required
overhead measurements, I typically
use measuring sticks, but when I
have a small piece it can be easier
to hold the material in place and
mark where it needs to be cut. To
hold the far end of the plywood as
I install it, I screw one of my all-
purpose L-shaped brackets to the
wall (about 1 in. below the frame
of the rake or eaves).

Installing Windows and Doors

For reasons I'll discuss in chapter 8,
I don't attempt to install large window and door units by myself. But
I routinely install single windows
and exterior doors. Before I pick up
the window or door, I set up a
bracket that holds the unit in the
opening yet permits movement as
I fine-tune the installation. I begin
by measuring the amount that the
trim or nailing flange sticks out
beyond the outside of the jambs

The All-Purpose Bracket

Several years ago I spent an hour or so fabricating four simple L-shaped brackets. I call these site-built brackets my "all-purpose brackets" because I use them for so many different jobs. I built them for a specific task, but after I had them for a while I discovered their hidden potential. When I built the brackets, I was in the midst of a kitchen remodel. I had to fabricate a custom countertop with a curved front edge, and I wanted something to hold the countertop securely upright as I applied a strip of laminate to the edge. The brackets worked like a charm.

In building the brackets, I knew I could use them for a similar task— holding doors on edge—but I had no idea how many other ways I'd end up using them. For instance, I screw the brackets to a standing wall and use them to hold up all manner of materials, including framing lumber, beams, plywood, drywall, exterior trim, and kitchen cabinets.

The brackets are easy to make, especially if you have a table saw set up on the job. I cut a scrap of ³/₄-in. *plywood into two rectangular pieces. One piece is 6 in. by 14 in., the other 6 in. by 14³/₄ in. Next I use my table saw to cut a ³/₄-in. groove (about ¹/₄ in. deep) down the center of each piece. I screw the pieces together in the shape of an L (with the 14³/₄-in. piece overlapping the 14-in. piece), then I cut a triangle-shaped brace with two 14-in. sides. To complete the bracket, I fit the brace in the grooves and secure it with a generous amount of glue and some screws.*

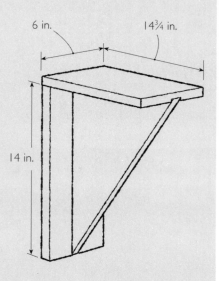

6 in. 14³/₄ in.

14 in.

Window-Setting Bracket

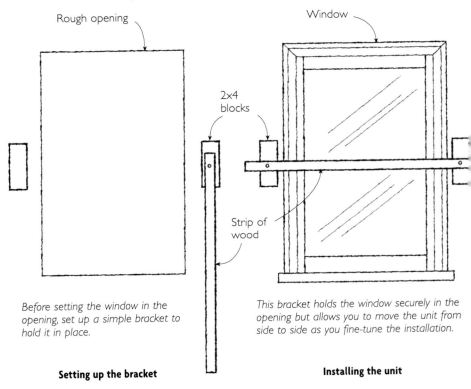

Rough opening

Window

2x4 blocks

Strip of wood

Before setting the window in the opening, set up a simple bracket to hold it in place.

Setting up the bracket

This bracket holds the window securely in the opening but allows you to move the unit from side to side as you fine-tune the installation.

Installing the unit

of the unit. I mark this amount on each side of the window opening, then nail a couple of 2x4 blocks about halfway up the opening and an inch or two beyond these marks.

After securing the blocks to the wall, I attach a strip of wood with one nail to one of the blocks (see the drawing above). I make sure that this strip, which can be anything from a 1x2 to a 2x4, swings freely and spans across to the other block when I rotate it up into a horizontal position. Now I pick up the window or door, set it in the opening, swing the strip of wood up across the unit, and nail it to the block on the opposite side. The unit is loose in the opening, but the bar keeps it securely in place. And, if I want, I can take a coffee break before finishing the installation.

Shingling the Roof

Roofing crews typically work as a team when they lay out the roof, but after striking the lines each roofer usually takes a section and works by himself. They do this because installing shingles is basically a one-man job. The layout is a different matter, though, and without a second pair of hands it can drag on.

The main challenge for the solo roofer is to streamline the layout. I do three things to get the layout completed in a reasonable amount of time. First, I use a 72-in. aluminum measuring stick. This ruler lies flat on the deck and is easy to maneuver with one hand. And, at 72 in., it's exactly twice the width of a standard shingle (see the drawing on p. 92). This means that I can mark it end-for-end to see how my vertical coursing will end up on the far side of the roof; or, in some cases, I can move the bond layout from the right to left side of the

roof if an interruption like a dormer prevents me from laying out the roof along the left side.

After marking the layout on the roof, I work with an economy of motion as I snap the chalklines. To hold the string, I drive nails halfway in along one side of the layout. I secure the string to the first nail and strike the line, but for subsequent lines I do not reattach the string to each nail. Instead, I loop the string over the nails. Also, I don't waste time reeling in the string to rechalk it; instead, I use a cube of red chalk, which I rub across the outstretched string with my left hand as I pull it taut with my right. To mark the rake of the roof (before cutting), I make a short slit in the top shingle, slip the end of the chalkline into the slit, pull the string down to the bottom of the rake, and snap the line.

The other thing I do to streamline the process is to use a gauged roofing hammer. The gauge on the hammer is 5 in. from the head of the hammer. To get the required 5-in. exposure for the shingles, I hook the gauge on the course I've just installed, then line up the shingle on the head of the hammer. I don't install the entire roof this way because roofs installed without any layout lines inevitably end up with wavy courses. I use a combination of layout lines and gauged

Streamlining Shingle Layout

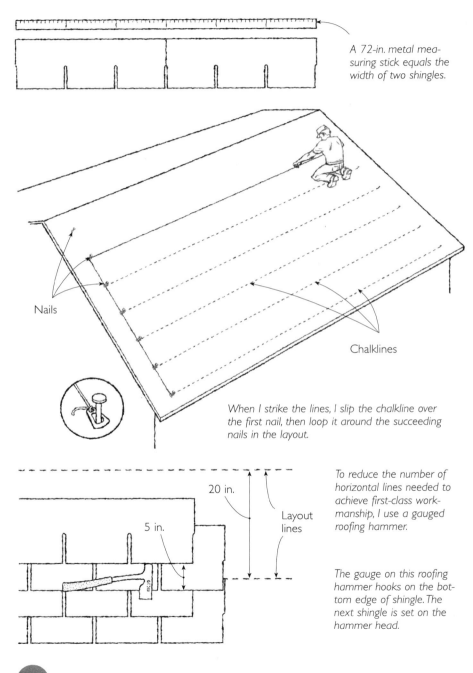

A 72-in. metal measuring stick equals the width of two shingles.

Nails

Chalklines

When I strike the lines, I slip the chalkline over the first nail, then loop it around the succeeding nails in the layout.

20 in.

Layout lines

5 in.

To reduce the number of horizontal lines needed to achieve first-class workmanship, I use a gauged roofing hammer.

The gauge on this roofing hammer hooks on the bottom edge of shingle. The next shingle is set on the hammer head.

courses. Typically, I snap layout lines every 20 in., which means that I use the gauge for three courses, then return to the layout on the fourth course.

Installing Wood Siding

Installing wood siding is considerably more challenging for the solo builder than shingling a roof. It's not too difficult to see why: The materials are long and are installed on a vertical surface; much of the work has to be completed standing on scaffolding; and every piece has to be cut and fit neatly into an existing space. Yet this job is quite manageable for one person. Over the years, I've discovered a number of commonsense approaches and simple tools and jigs that make running siding by myself an enjoyable process.

As always, I set up good scaffolding. Once it's set up I can work quickly and safely through the rest of the job.

Another thing that makes the siding go smoothly is careful layout. Before I begin the siding, I strike two reference lines. The first is about ½ in. above the tops of the windows; the second is about ¾ in. below the bottom of the sheathing (see the drawing on p. 95). The next step is to drive a nail halfway in on the upper layout line. I take a long, straight strip of wood, butt it against the nail, and mark it at the bottom reference line. I bring this strip of wood over to my work table and divide the distance between the two lines into equal increments. Each increment represents a course of siding.

To get equal increments, I use a divider—a device that looks and works much like a compass. When I divide the space, I start with a target increment, which is usually 6 in. for wood siding. The object is to get an even spacing that's as close to 6 in. as possible. To

Safely Stacking Siding across Scaffolding *Siding that is placed across a section of scaffolding looks a lot like a scaffold plank and presents a serious hazard. If you're not concentrating, you can mistakenly step on the siding, which can't support your weight. Where possible, keep the siding on the ground and lean it against the scaffold to keep it within reach. As you move higher up the wall, you can either stack the siding above the level you're walking on or make sure it rests on solid scaffolding planks.*

achieve this goal, I set the spread of the divider to 6 in., march it end-for-end up the wood strip, and see if it is running long or short (see the drawing below). I adjust the spread of the divider accordingly and march it up the span again. I repeat this process until I get the divider to land on the mark—at which point I know I have the space evenly divided.

Now I march the divider up the strip one more time, this time marking the increments as I go. I use this marked strip of wood as a story pole for installing the siding courses. By taking the time to adjust the courses slightly, I've produced a layout that ensures that a full piece of siding will run over the windows. This trick saves time, makes it easier to flash the top of the window, and produces a better-looking job.

How I mark the courses depends on the quality of the siding. If the siding is straight and consistent in width, I move the layout up to the tops of the courses. To do this, I take a scrap of the siding, hold the bottom of it even with the upper reference line, and scribe along the top of the scrap. After doing this at each end of the wall and at the ends of each space between the windows, I drive nails halfway in at the new marks. I can now lay out the tops of the courses by butting the story pole against the nails and transferring the layout to the wall (see the story pole to the left of the window in the drawing on the facing page). After marking the courses, I snap lines using the same basic technique I used on the roof.

Dividing a Distance into Equal Increments

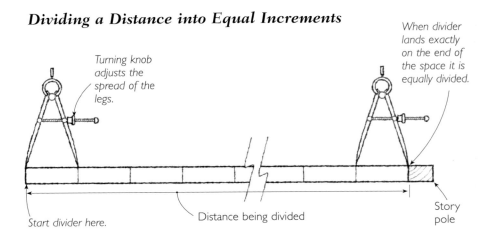

Turning knob adjusts the spread of the legs.

When divider lands exactly on the end of the space it is equally divided.

Start divider here.

Distance being divided

Story pole

Not all wood siding is straight enough to be installed along layout lines representing the top of the course. Cheap siding often has a gnarled top edge (it doesn't show after it's installed), which makes it difficult or impossible to follow a top line for layout. Also, if the siding is inconsistent in size, all the inconsistency shows if you follow lines along the top of the courses. Conversely, all the inconsistency is buried if you follow lines at the bottom of the courses. That's because the bottom of each siding course overlaps the top of the preceding course.

To lay out along the bottom, each line has to be snapped—one at a

Laying Out Lap Siding

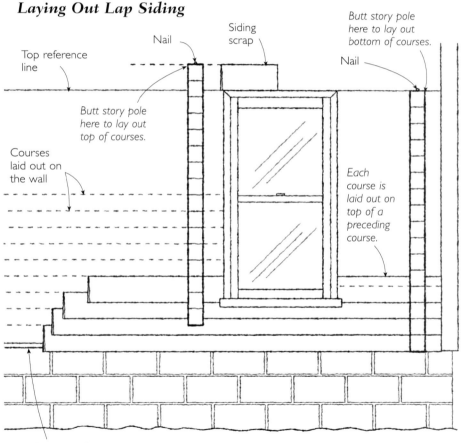

Top reference line

Nail

Siding scrap

Butt story pole here to lay out bottom of courses.

Nail

Butt story pole here to lay out top of courses.

Courses laid out on the wall

Each course is laid out on top of a preceding course.

Bottom reference line

Using a Modified Chalkline

By removing the hook at the end of a chalkline and replacing it with a block of wood, you can strike lines without puncturing the siding.

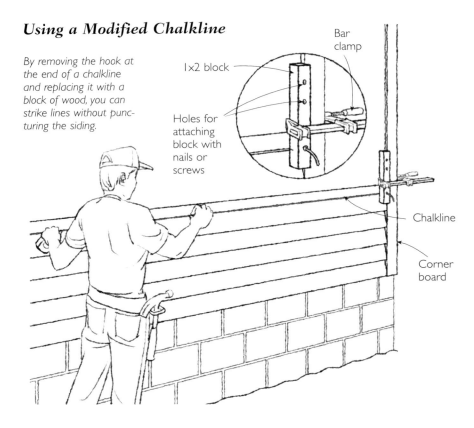

Bar clamp

1x2 block

Holes for attaching block with nails or screws

Chalkline

Corner board

time—on top of the course just installed. Hence, the course layout is an ongoing process that occurs during the installation. After installing each piece of siding, I butt the story pole against the nail installed at the original reference line, then transfer the layout from the pole to the wall (see the story pole to the right of the window in the drawing on p. 95).

I don't use a nail to hold the chalk-line as I snap the course line. It's

not a good practice to nail through the upper part of the siding, and leaving a nail hole is completely undesirable. Instead of nailing into the top of the siding, I use my modified chalkline, which has a block of wood instead of a hook at the end (see the drawing above). I can usually clamp the line in place by clamping the block to the window trim or to the corner board. If this is not practical, I attach the block to the wall by nail-ing in the area above the siding.

After I finish the layout, I begin cutting and fitting the siding. I rarely measure the spaces on the wall; instead I hold each piece in place and mark it directly. When I need to mark a group of pieces about the same size (when siding between two windows, for example), I cut several pieces a couple of inches longer than the space. Then I go to the layout and mark a piece for every line. By keeping these pieces in order, I get good custom fits that accurately reflect the slight variations in the width of the space. At the same time, I save several trips to the saw. It's another case of measure once and cut twice.

Because siding is fairly light, I can usually hang short pieces of siding without using a bracket to hold up the far end of the board. For long pieces, though, I often find it necessary to use a J-shaped bracket, which I scrounged from a previous job. If you don't have a ready-made bracket, it's easy to fabricate one out of a strip of mild steel about ⅛ in. thick by 1½ in. wide. Most hardware stores carry a selection of steel bars and rods.

The bracket I use is several inches longer than the width of the siding (usually 7½ in.). I hang the bracket in place with one or two nails, driven halfway in toward the top of the bracket (I drilled holes in the bracket for this purpose). These nails end up above the top of the siding I'm installing, and they're easy to remove once the siding is secured.

Bracket for Holding Siding

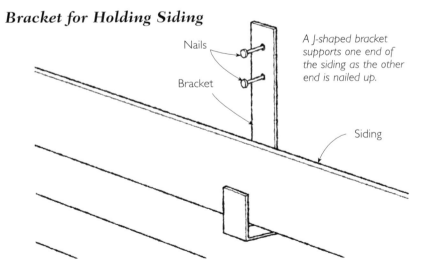

Nails

Bracket

A J-shaped bracket supports one end of the siding as the other end is nailed up.

Siding

While roofers and siders are still working on the outside of a house or addition, special trade contractors—electricians, plumbers, mechanical contractors, and others—often begin lacing wires, pipes, and ductwork through the skeleton of the structure. At this critical period in the project, the house is protected from the weather but the inside of the frame remains open and accessible.

After the special trade contractors finish installing the inner workings of their systems, the builder can install insulation in the floors, walls, and ceilings. Then it's time to hang drywall and to begin finishing the inside surfaces of the house. This is the final stretch of the job, where the building project visibly becomes a home.

Scores of interior materials need to be installed, but this discussion has to be limited. I won't go into mechanical, electrical, and plumbing work because in most areas such work has to be completed by licensed contractors. I'm not permitted by law to do this work for my customers, and I always hire it out to licensed contractors. There are other jobs that I'm allowed to do but choose not to. In chapter 8, I'll describe those jobs and explain why or when I pass them off to trusted subcontractors.

Even with the valuable help I get from my subcontractors, I still do a large portion of the interior work on projects myself. I often install the insulation, hang and finish the drywall, and, with the exception of hardwood floors, do the interior carpentry myself. I also do my own tile work. As different as these materials are, the problems I run into as a solo builder are remarkably similar to those discussed in earlier chapters. I have to come up with a way to measure across open spaces by myself, and I have to transfer those measurements quickly and accurately to the materials. I also have to find a way to hold the materials as I cut and install them.

As you'll see, I often solve these problems by going to my well-worn bag of tricks and pulling out

another version of the same proven methods I describe elsewhere in this book. But I can't rely entirely on these tried-and-true methods. The conditions and materials change in this stretch of the job, and I sometimes have to make corresponding adjustments to my techniques. In some situations, an adjustment is not enough, and I have to find an entirely new approach or make use of clever new tools.

In this chapter I'll describe how I install five different kinds of interior materials. I won't get into jobs that are obviously easy to do alone (installing insulation, finishing drywall, painting). I've arranged the topics in the same basic order that I do them on my jobs. But unlike many of the other chapters, where the topics are interrelated and the sequence of installation is such an important part of the process, the techniques described here are not closely connected. On many houses, in fact, these jobs are completed by five different subcontractors.

Hanging Drywall

On small additions, I usually hang and finish the drywall myself. By far the biggest challenge is hanging the ceiling. Not only are the sheets heavy and unwieldy, but they are also flimsy and easy to break. In a few cases, I've managed to man-

Using a Drywall Lift

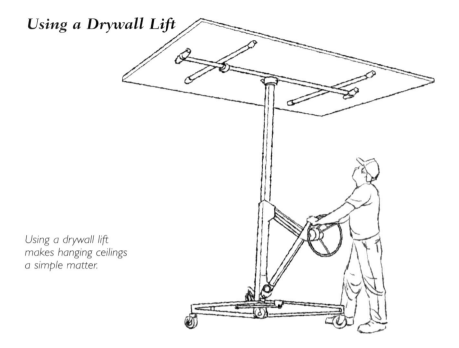

*Using a drywall lift
makes hanging ceilings
a simple matter.*

handle a full 8-ft. sheet of drywall onto a ceiling by myself, but I've never even attempted a 12-ft. sheet. In the past, when I got to the drywall phase of the job, I simply lined up a helper for a few hours to get the ceilings hung. But this proved expensive, and it caused delays because I had to hold off on drywalling until someone was available to help.

To solve this problem, I invested in a drywall lift. The drywall lift is a heavy-duty, telescoping jack made specifically for lifting and holding drywall and other large panels. It can be helpful for walls, but its primary purpose is to hoist sheets of drywall to the ceilings. The model I have raises the panel up to 11 ft. off the floor, and it can be modified for ceilings up to 15 ft. high.

Before hoisting the sheet of drywall into position, it has to be cut to fit. To measure the space, I face a familiar problem. As we've seen, a tape measure is about as effective for measuring across long, open spaces as a tennis racket is for paddling a canoe. Instead of using a floppy tape measure, I use measuring sticks for these overhead measurements.

For longer measurements, I use a strip of wood cut to exactly 100 in.

Measuring a Ceiling for Drywall

Cut a strip of wood exactly 100 in. long and use it to measure and mark the first 100 in. Then measure the balance of the distance with a manufactured measuring stick to get the exact measurement.

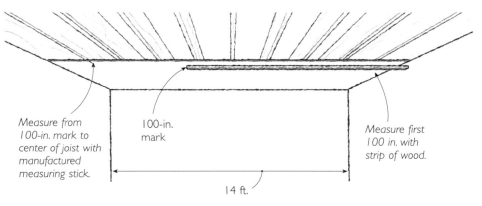

Measure from 100-in. mark to center of joist with manufactured measuring stick.

100-in. mark

Measure first 100 in. with strip of wood.

14 ft.

After butting one end of this 100-in. measuring stick against the wall (or, in some cases, against the edge of the previous sheet of drywall), I mark flush with the other end of the stick. Then I measure the balance of the space with one of my metal measuring sticks. Adding that dimension to the 100-in. measurement gives me the total measurement. I use this combination of sticks because it's easy to add the second measurement to a first measurement of 100 and come up with the total quickly.

Transferring the measurements to the drywall panels is not difficult for one person to do; in most cases, you can hook a tape measure over the edge and measure in the standard manner. Measuring sticks can also be used to measure the locations of light fixtures, vents, and other items in the ceiling. I often mark their positions directly onto a stick and transfer that measurement to the panel without ever knowing (or caring) what the dimension is.

Once the panel is cut, I use the lift to raise the sheet to the ceiling. Then I roll the lift to get the sheet close to its proper position. After locking the wheels of the lift, I climb up a stepladder and slide the sheet precisely into place before I

Enlarging a Door-Knob

Hole *To control the drill as you enlarge an existing hole in a door, use a scrap of wood to guide the bit. First bore the desired hole size through the scrap. Then clamp the scrap to the door with the hole positioned exactly where you want to bore the hole. The prebored scrap will guide the drill smoothly into the door.*

screw it tight. A lift costs several hundred dollars, but it has been an excellent investment for me. The first time I used it was on a large remodeling project in an older home with 10-ft. ceilings. On that job alone, I saved about $100 in labor.

Hanging drywall on walls is hard work but I've never found it to be particularly challenging to do by myself. If you find it difficult to control the upper piece as you install it, however, you can use an all-purpose bracket to support one

Holding a Door

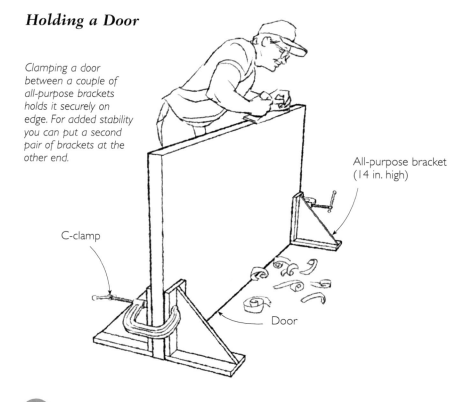

Clamping a door between a couple of all-purpose brackets holds it securely on edge. For added stability you can put a second pair of brackets at the other end.

All-purpose bracket (14 in. high)

C-clamp

Door

end while you attach the other. (Use the same basic technique described in the section on installing plywood to a standing wall in chapter 3.)

Working on Doors

When you hang prehung doors, you install the jamb and door as a unit. You don't need to cut or plane the door, the hinges are already in place, and the door and jamb are bored and ready to accept knobs and locksets. On many remodeling and repair jobs, though, you have to hang doors on existing door jambs. When you do this, you need to carefully trim and plane the door to fit the existing opening. Then you need to bore the door for knobs and locksets and cut mortises for the hardware. Finally, you must install the knobs, locksets, and hinges.

To do this persnickety and unforgiving work and at the same time retain my sanity, I use a couple of tricks to hold the door securely in place as I work. When I'm trimming the door with my circular saw, I need to hold the door flat. That's easy—I just clamp it across a couple of sawhorses. But when I'm planing the edge of the door, boring the door for knobs and locksets, mortising the edges for hinges and lock faces, and installing hardware, I need to hold the door

securely on edge. There are several commercially available brackets that are designed specifically for this purpose, but they are not necessary. By clamping the door between a pair or two of all-purpose brackets, I can hold the door every bit as securely as I could by using a commercial bracket. The only difference is that my site-built brackets are free.

Running Trim

Interior trim should fit tightly and neatly together, so measurement mistakes even as small as $1/16$ in.

Cutting Small Pieces of Trim *Using power tools to trim small pieces of wood is dangerous. It's difficult to hold a small piece securely, and if the revolving blade gets bound in the kerf, it can grab the piece and hurl it at the speed of a major league fastball. This careening chunk of wood is a hazard in its own right, but the fact that your hand might be pulled into the path of the blade is an even greater concern. Don't take a chance. If you cut a small piece of trim a bit too long, throw it away and try again using a longer—and safer—piece of material.*

Strategies for Measuring Walls for Trim

*There are two basic ways to mark trim to length quickly
and accurately when you're working alone.*

Option 1
Where possible, mark the material in place.

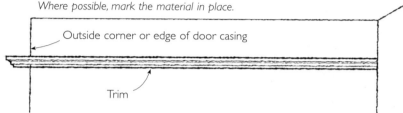

Outside corner or edge of door casing

Trim

Option 2
*For inside-to-inside measurements, use
a combination of measuring sticks.*

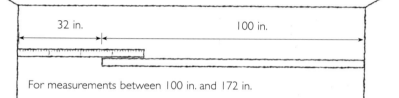

32 in.

100 in.

For measurements between 100 in. and 172 in.

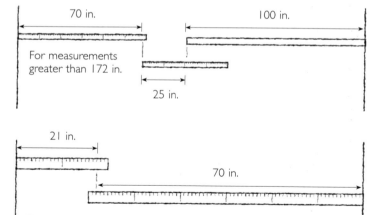

70 in.

100 in.

For measurements
greater than 172 in.

25 in.

21 in.

70 in.

For measurements less than 100 in.

can ruin a trim installation. If you're working alone, it's essential to come up with a way to make quick, accurate measurements. In many circumstances you can side-step this issue because many of the pieces of trim that go into a house can be held in place and marked directly. Whenever I can, I start with a rough preliminary measurement and cut the material a few inches long. I hold the piece in place and mark it, then cut it to fit. To do this, I need to be able to run the trim past the end of the space, as when I'm fitting the material to an outside corner of the wall or to the side of a door casing.

When I measure from one inside corner to another on the wall or near the ceiling, however, I can't let the piece run long, so I have to measure the space. To measure along the floor for base molding, I can use my tape measure. But to measure along the wall for chair rail or crown molding, I need the rigidity of measuring sticks. As I've done in other situations, I use a site-built 100-in. measuring stick. I push one end of the stick against the corner of the space I'm measuring and mark even with the other end. Then I measure from the other corner to the mark with a manufactured metal measuring stick. Adding 100 in. to the second measurement gives the length of the space.

My longest metal measuring stick is 72 in. If I have a space that exceeds 172 in. (14 ft. 4 in.), I make the first measurement with my 100-in. stick the same way. But I won't be able to span the remaining distance with my 72-in.-long metal stick, so instead I mark the second measurement from the corner at 70 in., then measure the distance between the two marks. Adding the last measurement to 170 gives me the length of the space. To measure a space just under 100 in., I would use the

Supporting a Chair Rail

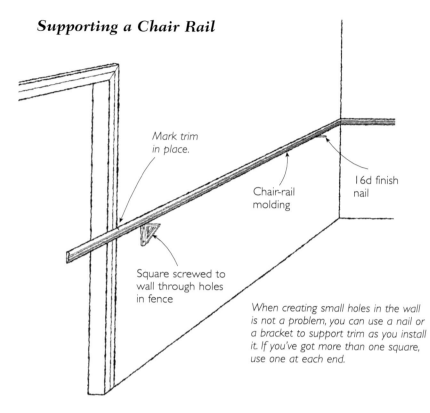

Mark trim in place.

Chair-rail molding

16d finish nail

Square screwed to wall through holes in fence

When creating small holes in the wall is not a problem, you can use a nail or a bracket to support trim as you install it. If you've got more than one square, use one at each end.

manufactured measuring stick to mark 70 in., then measure the balance. To transfer measurements to the trim stock, I use a tape measure. I can normally hook the tape on the end of the piece, but if the hook doesn't stay put, I use a spring clamp to hold it in place.

Trim stock is light, and I can often hold it in place as I mark or install it by pushing it horizontally into the opposite corner. This method becomes less effective, however, as the pieces get longer and heavier.

The position of the piece also affects the degree of difficulty; generally, the higher the installation, the more difficult it is to apply the necessary lateral pressure. When I install crown molding, for example, I'm typically working off a stepladder and can apply only a small amount of lateral pressure. When I'm standing on the floor installing a chair rail, on the other hand, I can spread my legs, dig in my feet, and really push the piece into the corner.

Supports for Installing Trim

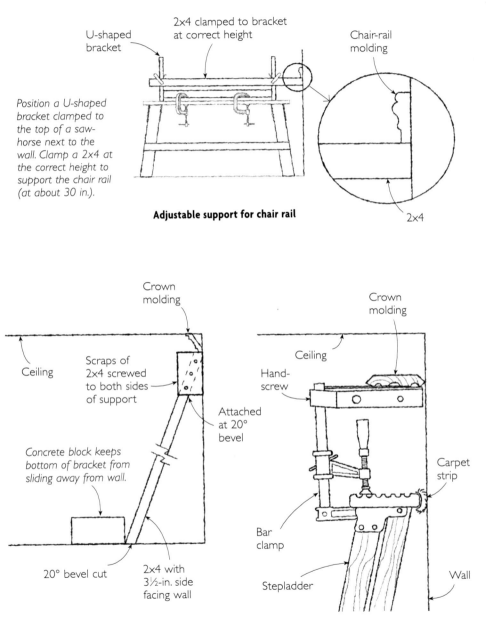

Position a U-shaped bracket clamped to the top of a saw-horse next to the wall. Clamp a 2x4 at the correct height to support the chair rail (at about 30 in.).

U-shaped bracket

2x4 clamped to bracket at correct height

Chair-rail molding

Adjustable support for chair rail

2x4

Crown molding

Ceiling

Scraps of 2x4 screwed to both sides of support

Concrete block keeps bottom of bracket from sliding away from wall.

Attached at 20° bevel

20° bevel cut

2x4 with 3½-in. side facing wall

Crown molding

Ceiling

Hand-screw

Carpet strip

Bar clamp

Stepladder

Wall

Supports for crown molding

Even when you're standing squarely on the floor, though, this technique has its limitations. You'll know it's not working when your workday begins to resemble a Laurel and Hardy routine, where the piece falls every time you get ready to mark or install it. The solution to this problem can be as simple as a 16d finish nail. After marking where the bottom of the molding will be, you can drive the nail partway in at that mark. The nail holds up one end of the piece while you mark or install the other. If you want to make your life even easier, put in a nail about 16 in. from each end of the space to support both ends of the trim.

I've used finishing nails to good effect for years but recently I discovered an even better way to support the molding. Instead of a nail, I now use a Swanson Mag Square. Screwing the square to the wall takes just a few seconds, yet it creates a firmer and larger support than a nail provides (see the drawing on p. 106). I have two of these squares, so I often put one near each end of the space.

The downside to using either of these methods is that they leave holes in the wall. I consider this a minor problem when I'm planning to paint or paper the walls. Drywall is a forgiving material, and it's easy to fill and repair the holes after I complete the trim. There have been occasions, though, when I've installed trim on walls that were finished, in which case leaving exposed holes is not acceptable.

To avoid making holes while installing chair-rail molding, I set up an adjustable support (see the top drawing on p. 107). After marking the height of the bottom of the chair rail on the wall, I position a sawhorse perpendicular to the wall, then clamp a U-bracket to the top of the sawhorse (see the sidebar on the facing page). Now, as I hold a 2x4 that touches the wall at the mark, I clamp it to the uprights of the U-bracket.

To support the far end of crown molding during installation, I use another support. This support consists of a 2x4 leaned against the wall with a couple of 2x4 blocks screwed to the top (see the bottom left drawing on p. 107). The 2x4 blocks serve as a shelf to support the crown as I install it. To keep this assembly from sliding down the wall, I place a toolbox or a concrete block at its base.

Another option is to lean a stepladder against the wall, then clamp a bar clamp to the top step (see the bottom right drawing on p. 107). Clamp a handscrew to the bar of the clamp at the correct height to support the crown molding. The

The U-Shaped Bracket

For years I've used two things to overcome the problems of working outside over the uneven ground: a good pair of sawhorses and a combination of stakes and batter boards. A few years ago I discovered a way to combine these two systems. In searching for something to support long boards as I cut them with my sliding compound miter saw, I came up with a simple U-shaped bracket. Clamping this bracket (which I made out of 2x4s) to the top of my sawhorse gave me a pair of sturdy uprights. On these uprights I clamped a 2x4 crossbar even with the table of my saw.

The support worked like a charm, and I soon discovered that I could use this portable and adjustable rig for other jobs. I also use it to support lumber as I install it, to make a batter board, and to provide a place on which to hook my tape measure. To lend stability to the U-shaped bracket, I sometimes place a couple of concrete blocks on the shelf of the sawhorse.

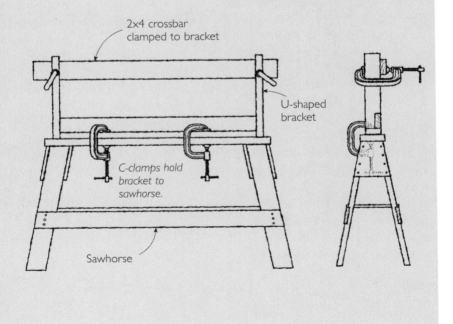

2x4 crossbar clamped to bracket

U-shaped bracket

C-clamps hold bracket to sawhorse.

Sawhorse

possible configurations of jury-rigged brackets for this job are limited only by your imagination.

Hanging Wall Cabinets

Kitchen cabinets are not terribly heavy, and with a little planning it's not too difficult to hang them by yourself. There are at least three good ways to approach this task. The first approach is to screw a pair of all-purpose brackets to the wall and rest the cabinet on the brackets as you install it. After the first cabinet is secured to the wall, clamp a scrap of wood to the underside of the cabinet, extending the scrap a few inches beyond the side. This scrap serves as a shelf to support and help align the next cabinet. To install the next cabinet, I often use a combination of this shelf at one end and a single all-purpose bracket at the other (see the top drawing on the facing page).

If you object to the screw holes that this method leaves in the wall, you can use another approach. Install the base cabinets first, then set a site-built stand on top of the lower units. Making the stand ¼ in. shorter than the desired height of the wall cabinets permits the use of shims to precisely adjust the final height of the cabinet.

The third approach to hanging wall cabinets is to use a cabinet jack.

The T-Jak is a tool specifically designed to help solo builders hold up cabinets during installation. This jack can be quickly and finely adjusted by turning a threaded knob. The standard T-Jak has a lifting range of 53 in. to 84 in., but with optional extensions it can be used to support material at higher levels. For those who like to hang wall cabinets after installing the base cabinets, there's also a Mini Brute T-Jak, which is designed for holding cabinets 15 in. to 24 in. above the base cabinets.

The T-Jak can be used to support other materials (such as drywall for ceiling installation), and it can be used effectively as a spreader. It's a simple, well-conceived tool with an agreeable price tag. You can get the standard T-Jak for the price of a good drill. If you're a full-time kitchen installer, you might be interested in another cabinet hoist called the Lightning Lift. This rig is quite a bit more expensive than the T-Jak, but it's a heavier tool with wheels. You can use it to lift and move several cabinets at the same time.

Squaring Up a Large Tile Layout

Setting tile is very much a one-man job. The only part of this job that I've found challenging to do by myself is the process of squaring

Supporting Wall Cabinets

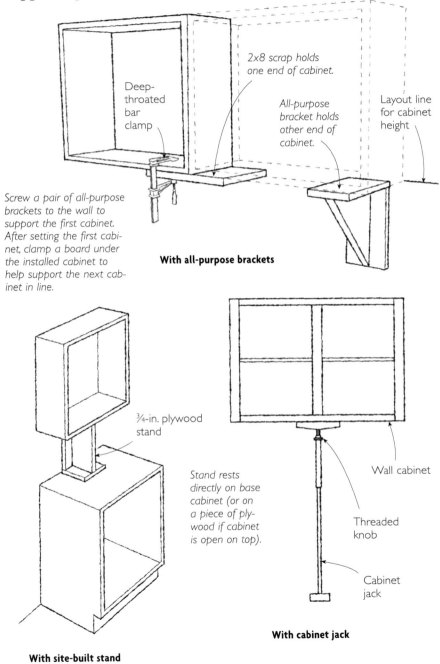

2x8 scrap holds
one end of cabinet.

Deep-
throated
bar
clamp

All-purpose
bracket holds
other end of
cabinet.

Layout line
for cabinet
height

*Screw a pair of all-purpose
brackets to the wall to
support the first cabinet.
After setting the first cabinet, clamp a board under
the installed cabinet to
help support the next cabinet in line.*

With all-purpose brackets

¾-in. plywood
stand

*Stand rests
directly on base
cabinet (or on
a piece of ply-
wood if cabinet
is open on top).*

Wall cabinet

Threaded
knob

Cabinet
jack

With cabinet jack

With site-built stand

up a large layout. In chapter 2, we examined how to square up foundations using the Pythagorean Theorem. When you square up a tile layout, you can apply the same technique. Use the length and width of the layout to calculate the hypotenuse of a right triangle, then pull that dimension diagonally across the layout to square it up. This technique works, but there is an easier way to square up a tile layout—one that uses geometry in a manner that takes advantage of the circumstances of tile work.

Whether you're tiling a wall or a floor, you begin the layout on a flat surface. This is a lot easier than laying out a foundation over uneven ground. But you've still got one problem—you have nothing to hook your tape measure to. The solution is to use a measuring stick. In this situation, though, the measuring stick is more than a solution; it's part of a new and better method for squaring up the layout.

By using a measuring stick as a beam compass, you can quickly and easily lay out a perfect right angle—without making precise, time-consuming measurements. What's more, this right angle can be drawn out in the middle of the layout. This option makes the technique well suited to tile work, which usually proceeds from the inside of the layout toward the perimeter.

To show you how I lay out tile, I'll use the layout of a large tile floor as an example. I start by marking a baseline down the length of the room. To lay out the position of this line, which I'll call the primary baseline, I find the center of the space at each end of the room. I mark both ends, but for testing the layout I'll work from only one mark.

After marking the center, I lay out the tiles dry from this point across the width of the room to see whether this starting point yields a narrow course at the edges.

Avoiding Narrow Courses of Tile

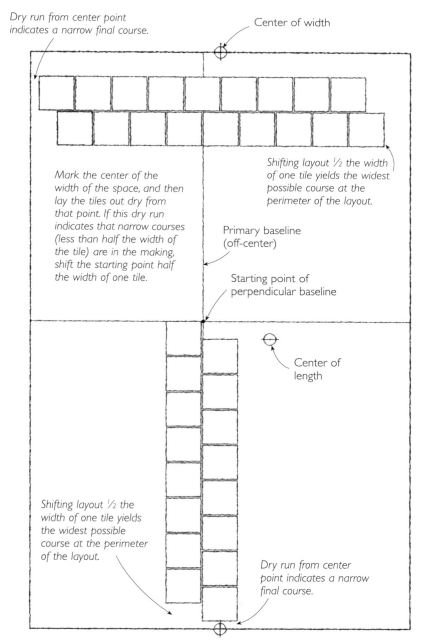

Dry run from center point indicates a narrow final course.

Center of width

Mark the center of the width of the space, and then lay the tiles out dry from that point. If this dry run indicates that narrow courses (less than half the width of the tile) are in the making, shift the starting point half the width of one tile.

Shifting layout ½ the width of one tile yields the widest possible course at the perimeter of the layout.

Primary baseline (off-center)

Starting point of perpendicular baseline

Center of length

Shifting layout ½ the width of one tile yields the widest possible course at the perimeter of the layout.

Dry run from center point indicates a narrow final course.

Laying Out the Perpendicular Baseline

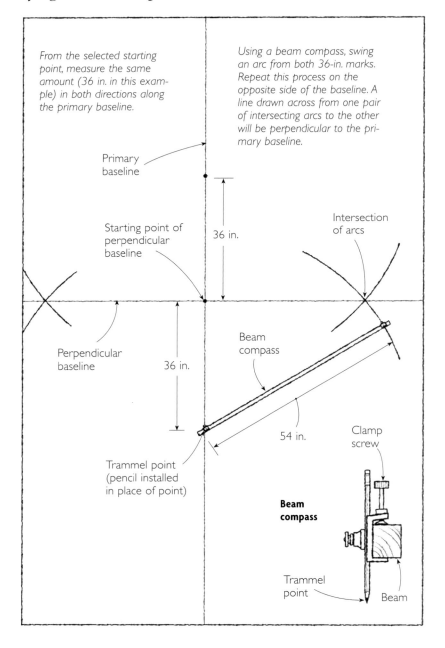

From the selected starting point, measure the same amount (36 in. in this example) in both directions along the primary baseline.

Using a beam compass, swing an arc from both 36-in. marks. Repeat this process on the opposite side of the baseline. A line drawn across from one pair of intersecting arcs to the other will be perpendicular to the primary baseline.

Primary baseline

Starting point of perpendicular baseline

Intersection of arcs

36 in.

Perpendicular baseline

Beam compass

36 in.

54 in.

Clamp screw

Trammel point (pencil installed in place of point)

Beam compass

Trammel point

Beam

(I strive to avoid narrow courses for two reasons: first, because they're hard to cut and install and, second, because they offend the eye.) If this "dry run" yields unsightly narrow courses (i.e., less than half the width of the tile), I shift the entire layout one half the width of the tile and make new marks. This adjustment produces the largest possible courses at the ends of the layout.

As soon as I'm satisfied with this portion of the layout, I snap a chalkline from mark to mark down the length of the room. I usually use a nail to hold the far end of the chalkline as I strike the line. But if there's a cement base on the floor, I prefer not to drive a nail through it. Instead, I loop the string around a flat, heavy object, such as concrete block or a toolbox. With the string anchored on the mark at one end, I pull to the mark at the other end and snap the line.

After snapping this primary baseline, I lay out the position of a perpendicular baseline. To do this, I mark the center of the room as measured along the primary baseline. Once again, I lay out the tiles dry, this time in a line that runs vertically along the primary baseline. If this dry run reveals that I'll end up with narrow courses, I shift the layout half the width of one tile.

After determining where I want the perpendicular baseline to begin, I measure and mark it on the floor. It's imperative to get this second baseline precisely perpendicular to the primary baseline; otherwise the tile courses will rack as you install them and end up looking amateurish. To ensure that the perpendicular baseline runs out at a 90° angle from the primary baseline, I start by making two equal-distance marks out from the center along the baseline (see the drawing on the facing page). The exact length isn't important, but it's essential that both measurements be identical. For this example, let's use a 36-in. measuring stick. I place one end on the perpendicular baseline mark and mark the other end.

After making the marks in both directions, I use trammel points to set up a beam compass. Before making the beam compass, I remove the steel point from one of my trammels and replace it with a pencil. The exact length of this beam compass is not important, but I usually make it about 1½ times the length of the measurement I've just marked on the primary baseline. For this example, the beam compass would be 1½ times 36 in., or 54 in.

To make the beam compass, I clamp my trammel points about 54 in. apart on a 1x2 strip. This is a quick and dirty measurement because the exact length of the beam compass is not important. (If you don't own a pair of trammel points, you can make a site-built beam compass in a few minutes; see the box on p. 115.)

To use the beam compass, I set the end of one trammel point into one of the 36-in. marks and use it as a pivot to swing an arc, as shown in the drawing on p. 114. At the other end of the compass a pencil draws the arc on the floor. I repeat the process at the other 36-in. mark, pushing the trammel in at the mark, swinging the compass, and drawing the arc. The point where these two arcs intersect is the critical point I need for this layout. A line extended from this point of intersection to the center perpendicular baseline mark on the primary baseline will be perpendicular to the primary baseline.

To lay out a perpendicular line to the opposite side of the primary baseline, I swing a second pair of arcs on that side. Typically, I swing a pair of intersecting arcs on both sides of the primary baseline, then snap a line between their points of intersection. It should pass right through the middle mark. The whole process takes just a few minutes, is very accurate, and is easy to do alone.

Building a deck is part foundation work, part frame carpentry, part finish carpentry. The job begins over the open ground, with no level or square surfaces to measure against. You have to develop these references from scratch, just as you do when laying out a foundation. Yet while deck layout is akin to the layout of a foundation, the materials are similar to those found in the frame of a house and require the skills of a frame carpenter. Unlike the frame of a house, though, the structure of a deck remains open to view when the job is done. Most of the deck consists of treated lumber, which has to be joined neatly together to satisfy aesthetic demands. This is the realm of a trim carpenter.

At first glance, this may not seem to be appropriate work for a solo builder. You have to install long, heavy timbers and pull measurements across broad, open spaces. Your work needs to be accurate and neat, and you need to finish the job in a reasonable amount of time. So is this suitable work for one person? I've built numerous decks by myself and made a living in the process, so my answer is yes. Aside from good layout and carpentry skills, the main things you need to build a deck solo are forethought—so the steps and materials are organized—and lots of clamps.

In this chapter, I'll walk you through the construction of a 12-ft. by 16-ft. deck. The deck will be a simple, rectangular, post-and-platform deck that's bolted to the house (see the middle example in the drawing on p. 121). I've built numerous decks like this, but it would be inaccurate to call it a typical deck. The size and design of decks vary considerably (see the sidebar on pp. 120-121 for a discussion of design variables). The variations in design, in turn, affect the choice of building techniques. Most of the principles set forth in this chapter can be used on any deck, but a few may have to be adjusted to meet the specific conditions of your job, like size and climate.

Outside Structure

When I lay out and build a deck, I violate the commonsense order of construction that has been summed up in the pithy expression "built from the ground up." To a certain degree, in fact, I build from the top down. The first thing I build is the outline of the frame, which I prop up on temporary supports. Then I use the frame to help lay out the positions of the footings. After I dig the footings, I attach the posts to the propped-up frame, with the bottoms of the posts suspended above the bottoms of the excavations. It's only after I've got the posts braced plumb that I mix the concrete for the footings, which I place under and around the base of the posts. This sequence might seem odd at first, but I've found that it's quick, accurate, and well suited to working without a helper.

Layout on the House

The first thing I do when I build a deck is mark where I want it to begin and end on the side of the house. After I mark the beginning point, I nail a 2x2 scrap there, hook my tape measure over the scrap, and pull the long measurement, which is 16 ft. in this example. Next, I remove the 2x2 and cut the siding out where I intend to attach the deck to the house. I also remove one piece of siding above

Band Layout

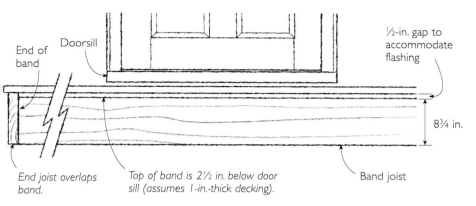

End of band

Doorsill

½-in. gap to accommodate flashing

8¾ in.

End joist overlaps band.

Top of band is 2½ in. below door sill (assumes 1-in.-thick decking).

Band joist

the top of the intended deck to make room for flashing. I know the top of the deck will be just below the threshold of the door, so it's easy to see which piece of siding to take out. For a freestanding deck, there's no need to cut and remove the siding.

The Band

The next step is to bolt the band joist of the deck to the house. On this deck, I'm using 2x10s for the band and all the other joists. To lay out the location of the band, I have to think ahead and decide how I want to do three things. First, I must decide the precise level I want the top of the finished deck to be. I typically put the top of the deck 1 in. down from the under-side of the doorsill. (In areas where heavy snow is expected, builders often set the deck a full step down from the doorsill.) So if I intend to

use 5/4 decking, which is a full 1 in. thick, I need to make the top of the joists 2 in. down from the underside of the doorsill.

I don't lay out the top of the band at that level, however, because of the second consideration: the flashing. I install the top of the band ½ in. lower than the top of the joists to accommodate the flashing. This technique prevents the problem of trapped water above the band and permits the water to flow off the flashing. (See "The Flashing" on p. 123 for more.) The correct elevation for the top of the band for this example is 2½ in. below the underside of the doorsill.

After striking a layout line at this height, I turn my attention to the third consideration: how I want to attach the end joists to the band.

Deck Design
Variables

In the simplest of terms a deck is an outdoor floor system. Because decks are made out of long, rigid pieces of lumber, the easiest—and cheapest—shape to build is the rectangle. In most cases, the width of the deck is limited by the span of the joists that make up the floor system.

To support your deck, you can make use of the house by bolting one side of the deck to it (top and middle examples in the drawing on the facing page). Although this widespread practice saves time and money, there is one good reason not to do it: Water can be trapped between the deck and the house.

If you decide to build the deck independent of the house, you have to build a structure to support the side of the deck adjacent to the house (the bottom example in the drawing). On the outside of the deck, you almost always have to build a supporting structure. Although you can use masonry piers to hold up the outside of the deck, the most common supporting systems are a post-and-beam structure under the floor

system (top example) or a series of posts set along the perimeter of the floor system (middle example).

When you cantilever the floor system over a post-and-beam structure, the deck takes on a contemporary look. Setting the posts along the outside edge, on the other hand, gives it a more traditional feel—particularly when the posts extend above the deck and become part of the balustrade.

The balustrade has an enormous impact on how a finished deck looks. To make a modern-looking balustrade, use a continuous top rail and let the balusters pass over the face of the perimeter joists. To make a traditional-looking balustrade, let some of the posts poke a couple of inches above the top rail and install post caps or finials on top of the posts. At the bottom, include a lower rail set 3 in. to 4 in. above the deck.

Types of Deck

Decks are often classified according to the way the joists are supported at each end.

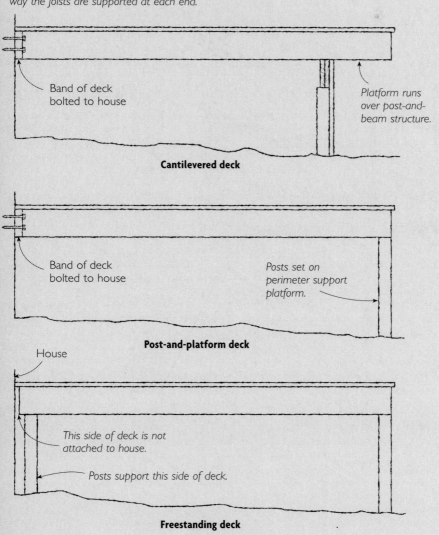

Band of deck bolted to house

Platform runs over post-and-beam structure.

Cantilevered deck

Band of deck bolted to house

Posts set on perimeter support platform.

Post-and-platform deck

House

This side of deck is not attached to house.

Posts support this side of deck.

Freestanding deck

To cover the end grain of the band, I like to lap the end joists over the band. This means I have to measure and mark 1½ in. in from each end of the deck layout (marked on the wall of the house) to determine the starting and ending points of the band.

I begin the installation of the band by cutting the 2x10 to length and width. The band needs to be 3 in. less than the 16-ft. length (192 in.) to accommodate the end joists, so I cut it 189 in. long. The band also needs to be ½ in. down from the top of the joists yet the bottoms must be even, so I rip ½ in. off the width to make the board 8¾ in. wide. To hold the far end of the band as I install it, I use an all-purpose bracket (see the sidebar on p. 89). Unfortunately, the bracket has to be affixed to the house below the floor frame.

Rather than try to screw the bracket into the masonry foundation, I nail a scrap of 2x lumber to the house so that it hangs down to accept the screws (see the drawing below). This scrap needs to be about 24 in.

Bracket for Installing the Band

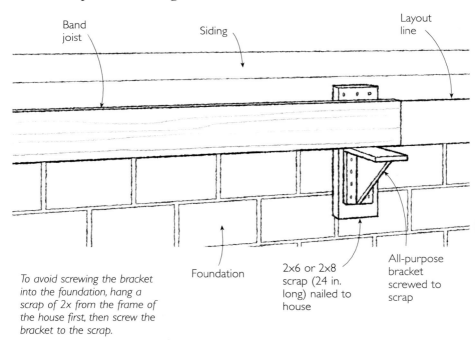

Band joist

Siding

Layout line

To avoid screwing the bracket into the foundation, hang a scrap of 2x from the frame of the house first, then screw the bracket to the scrap.

Foundation

2x6 or 2x8 scrap (24 in. long) nailed to house

All-purpose bracket screwed to scrap

long. I make it extend from a point about 2 in. above the layout line for the band to about 12 in. below the top of the foundation. Because the scrap must accommodate a 6-in.-wide bracket, I use a piece that's at least 5½ in. wide. By keeping the nails for this scrap in the area just above the layout line for the band, I can easily reach them later for removal. After I attach the scrap to the wall, I measure and mark 8¾ in. (the width of the band) down from the layout line. I screw the all-purpose bracket to the scrap so the top of the bracket is even with that mark.

I can now rest one end of the band on the bracket while I nail the other end in place along the layout line. After I've got five or six nails in the unsupported half of the band, I no longer need the bracket to hold up the band. I take the bracket off the scrap then remove the nails holding the scrap and slip it out from behind the band. Then I finish nailing the rest of the band. Once I have the band nailed in place, I bolt it to the house. In my area, the building code requires a ⅝-in. hot-dipped galvanized bolt every 20 in.

The Flashing

With the band bolted securely to the house, I turn my attention to one of the most important details of the job: the flashing. The purpose

Check for Wires before Drilling *Before you drill through the band and into the side of a house, go inside the basement or the crawl space of the house, peel back the insulation, and make sure there are no wires in the path of your drill bit. If you find wire (or ducts and pipes for that matter), consider drilling from the inside out.*

of flashing is to direct rainwater away from the house. Without flashing, water gets trapped between the band of the deck and the wall of the house. The consequences of that water can be devastating. It's imperative to provide a clear path for large amounts of water to flow off the flashing.

To protect the house from this moisture, I install aluminum or copper flashing bent in the shape of an L, with part of the horizontal leg of that L turned down (see the drawing on p. 125). The long vertical leg of this L is 3 in.; the horizontal base is 1½ in.; and the part that's bent down is 1 in. Because this profile is not commercially available, I have it made by a local commercial roofer.

Where Deck Meets House

The Achilles' heel of decks has historically been where the deck meets the house. When decks first became popular in the 1970s, carpenters typically just nailed a band to the house and built the deck out from that point. Unfortunately, some of those decks collapsed. To make matters worse, these catastrophic failures usually occurred at precisely the wrong place and time: on high decks, top-heavy with people.

The reason for these failures turned out to be the nails holding the band to the house. Typically the weight of the people—who in many cases were dancing—caused the deck to peel away from the house and come crashing down. Building officials responded to these failures by requiring that decks be bolted to the house and that posts over 4 ft. high be securely braced (to resist lateral forces).

These measures have removed the danger of sudden, catastrophic failure in decks. But in the meantime another problem at the house/deck juncture has become apparent. Water seeping between the band of the deck and the wall of the house causes the untreated wood on the house to gradually rot. This is a slow, insidious process, but once the damage is done it is very difficult—and expensive—to repair.

There are two simple ways to avoid this problem. The first is to carefully flash the house/band juncture. The second is to build the deck independent of the house. Designing and building a freestanding deck is more difficult than simply bolting one side of the deck to the house, but by leaving an open space between the house and the deck, you eliminate the problem of water trapped against the house.

To install the flashing, I place it on top of the band and nail through the top half of the tall, vertical leg into the house. The top half of the flashing will later be covered by the siding, so these nails will be protected from the weather and well above any sitting water. It's important to avoid nailing in the lower half of the flashing, where water flows and sometimes accumulates, because that water often finds its

Installing the Flashing

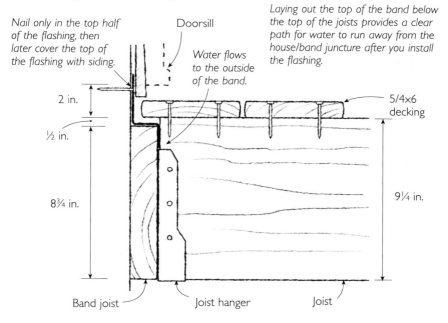

Nail only in the top half of the flashing, then later cover the top of the flashing with siding.

Doorsill

Laying out the top of the band below the top of the joists provides a clear path for water to run away from the house/band juncture after you install the flashing.

Water flows to the outside of the band.

2 in.

½ in.

8¾ in.

5/4x6 decking

9¼ in.

Band joist

Joist hanger

Joist

way to the nail holes and seeps under the flashing.

For a 16-ft. length, I have to use two pieces of flashing, which means I have to overlap the flashing several inches in the middle of the band. This seam is a vulnerable point in the flashing so I carefully seal it with high-quality caulk. I also take pains to seal the flashing well at the two ends of the deck.

The Frame

The next step is to install the two end joists. The first thing I do is set up a support to hold the end of the joist that's adjacent to the house.

I clamp a scrap of 2x4 (or 2x6) under the bottom of the band (the best clamp for this is a short pipe clamp equipped with Mastodon Jaw Extenders). Letting this scrap project a few inches past the end of the band creates a shelf to support the joist, as shown in the top drawing on p. 126.

To support the outboard end of the joist, I set up one of two possible rigs, both of which roughly resemble football goalposts. If the deck is going to be less than 4 ft. off the ground, I use a U-shaped bracket clamped to a sawhorse (see the sidebar on p. 109). If the deck is

Installing End Joists

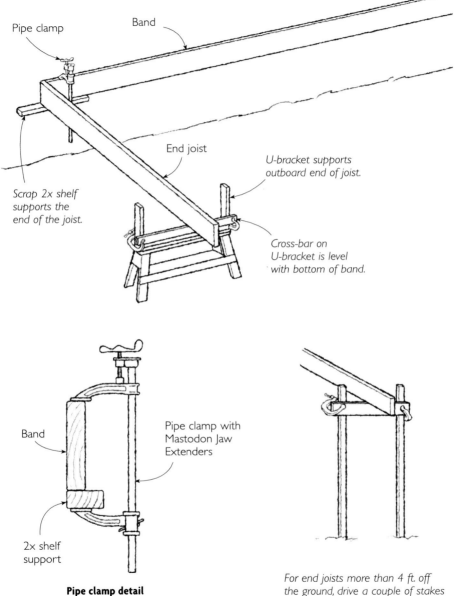

Pipe clamp

Band

End joist

U-bracket supports outboard end of joist.

Scrap 2x shelf supports the end of the joist.

Cross-bar on U-bracket is level with bottom of band.

Band

2x shelf support

Pipe clamp with Mastodon Jaw Extenders

Pipe clamp detail

For end joists more than 4 ft. off the ground, drive a couple of stakes into the ground for the uprights of the goalpost-shaped support.

Squaring the End Joist to the House

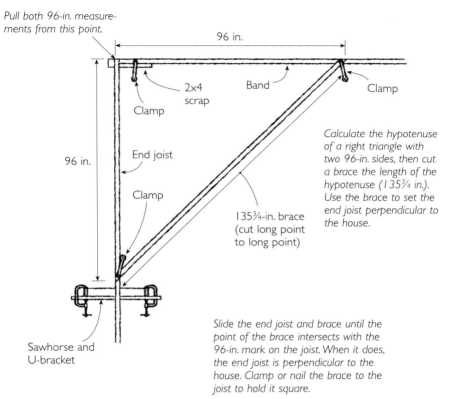

Pull both 96-in. measurements from this point.

96 in.

2x4 scrap

Clamp

Band

Clamp

96 in.

End joist

Clamp

135¾-in. brace (cut long point to long point)

Calculate the hypotenuse of a right triangle with two 96-in. sides, then cut a brace the length of the hypotenuse (135¾ in.). Use the brace to set the end joist perpendicular to the house.

Sawhorse and U-bracket

Slide the end joist and brace until the point of the brace intersects with the 96-in. mark on the joist. When it does, the end joist is perpendicular to the house. Clamp or nail the brace to the joist to hold it square.

more than 4 ft. off the ground, I drive a couple of long stakes into the ground and place a support in between (this rig looks like a batter board). I use my laser level to mark the uprights of the rig even with the underside of the band. (If you don't have a laser level, you can use a level and a straightedge.) Then I clamp a horizontal 2x4 from mark to mark. When I've completed my

goalpost-like support, I set the end joist in place and nail the end adjacent to the house into the side of the band.

The next task is to square the joist to the house. To do this I use the Pythagorean Theorem discussed in chapter 2. Instead of using strings to represent the sides of a right triangle, however, I use three boards.

Two of those boards—the band and the end joist—will be part of the permanent deck; the third, which represents the hypotenuse, is a temporary brace.

I calculate the hypotenuse of a triangle with two 96-in.-long sides. (The exact length of these sides is not crucial; I chose this length because it's half the length of the deck.)

$$\sqrt{2} \times 96 = 135.77 \text{ or } 135\frac{3}{4} \text{ in.}$$

After determining the hypotenuse, I hook my tape measure over the end joist and pull it along the band, measuring and marking 96 in. from the corner. Next I measure and mark 96 in. from the same corner along the outside edge of the joist. I now have the lengths of the two sides of my measuring triangle. Because the outboard end of the joist is simply resting on the goal-post rig, I can swing the joist laterally (like a hinge attached at the band) as I set it square to the band. Instead of using my tape measure to pull the hypotenuse as I brace the joist square to the house, I use the brace itself as a measuring stick.

I cut the brace exactly 135¾ in. long with 45° miters at each end (the 135¾-in. dimension is mea-

Installing the Rim Joist

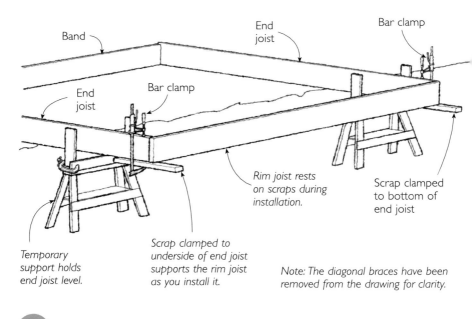

Band

End joist

Bar clamp

End joist

Bar clamp

Rim joist rests on scraps during installation.

Scrap clamped to bottom of end joist

Temporary support holds end joist level.

Scrap clamped to underside of end joist supports the rim joist as you install it.

Note: The diagonal braces have been removed from the drawing for clarity.

sured from long point to long point). Next I set the brace diagonally across from the corner formed by the band and the end joist and clamp it at the 96-in. mark on the band. Then, I move the joist and the brace until the long point of the brace intersects with the 96-in. mark on the joist. When these points intersect, the joist is perpendicular to the band, so I clamp the brace to the joist to hold it in place.

After repeating this process on the other end of the deck, I install the rim joist to complete the basic rec-

tangle of the deck. To hold the rim joist in place, I clamp 2x4 blocks under the end of each end joist, creating small shelves at both ends. Installing the rim joist is then a piece of cake, because both ends are supported. On some decks, I attach the rim joist temporarily, mark the footing locations, and then remove it while I'm digging the footings. (I often do this on low decks, where the rim joist would interfere with the digging.)

The Footings and Posts
The deck structure is now a level and square rectangle held up by

Quadruple-Duty Post

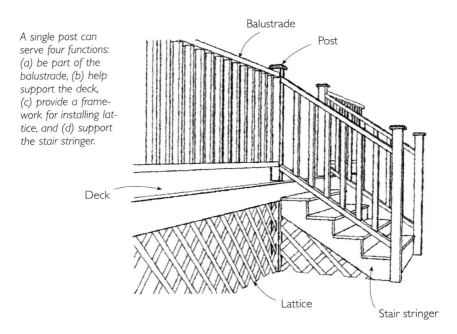

A single post can serve four functions: (a) be part of the balustrade, (b) help support the deck, (c) provide a framework for installing lattice, and (d) support the stair stringer.

Balustrade

Post

Deck

Lattice

Stair stringer

Laying Out Large Decks

The width of a deck is usually limited to the span of the joists (typically 16 ft. or less). The length of the deck, on the other hand, can easily be made as long as the house. To build a modest, 16-ft.-long deck, I use the rim joist both to lay out the locations of posts and to suspend the posts while I pour the concrete footings. But what do I do when I have to build a much longer deck, where the rim joist has to be pieced together from two or three boards? I use string.

After installing and squaring up both end joists as described in the text, I set up a string that extends from the top, outside corner of one end joist to the top, outside corner of the other. Next I hook my tape measure over one of the end joists and measure and mark the post locations on the string. (I mark the layout on the string with a felt-tipped marker; if the tape measure won't stay put on the joist, I clamp it down.) After transferring the layout from the string to the ground, I lay out and dig the footings.

The final step is to install the concrete footings and the posts. To do this, I work on one footing/post assembly at a time and save the post layout and cutting for later. I begin by mixing a batch of moist but stiff concrete. I pack 8 in. of this mixture in the bottom of the footing then set a post on the concrete. After making sure that the post will be long enough (39 in. above the string) to accommodate the balustrade, I brace it plumb in both directions and even with the marks on the string.

With the post securely braced, I pour a wet, mushy batch of concrete around the post until it's level with the surface of the ground. After the concrete cures, I cut the notch and the top of the post as it stands.

temporary supports. The next step is to install the permanent posts. I mark the location of the posts on the perimeter joists (the end joists and the rim joist), then transfer those locations to the ground with a plumb bob. Experience has taught me to think about more than just providing support for the deck when I plan the locations of the posts.

If I intend to underskirt the deck with lattice, for instance, I make sure the posts are no more than 8 ft. apart, which is the length of a sheet of lattice. If I'm going to build a set of stairs, I add a post to support each stringer. Finally, if I plan on having the posts extend through the deck and serve as newels for the balustrade, I make sure the posts are no more than 8 ft. apart. (Keeping the space between the newels under 8 ft. lessens the chances that the rails will sag or bow and provides for a strong, safe balustrade.) I often use the same post for all of these functions (see the drawing on p. 129).

After I determine where I want the posts, I mark their locations on the perimeter joists. This process is simply a matter of pulling the tape measure from the outside corners of the propped-up perimeter. Next I lower a plumb bob and transfer the layout to the ground. Based on this layout, I measure and mark the outline of each footing, which I make 16 in. square.

In my part of the country, the footings only need to be 20 in. deep to get below the frost line. The clay soil that predominates here yields readily to hand tools, so I rarely spend more than 30 minutes digging each footing by hand. When I'm done, the excavation is neat, with plumb sides, a flat bottom,

TRICKS OF THE TRADE

Digging Tools
When you dig the footings for a deck, the goal is not to move dirt—it's to carve a clean opening in the ground, with a level bottom and plumb sides. I've found that the best tools for this job are a small, square shovel, a one-hand mattock, and a couple of different-sized brick trowels. I also keep a large pair of loppers handy for cutting tree roots.

and no loose soil—the perfect form for the concrete. Having built as far north as Maine, however, I know that things aren't always so easy. If you live in a cold region and/or have to contend with difficult soil, you may want to use excavating equipment (see the sidebar on p. 132).

When I finish digging, I pour the footings and install the posts. I do these things at the same time, so the bottom of the post is embedded in the concrete. Although this practice is approved by most building codes, some carpenters object to it because they're concerned about the long-term effects of leaving the post in contact with the concrete. The main concern is that the base of the post will absorb moisture

Building Decks in Cold Climates

In cold climates, where the frost line is more than 3 ft. down, it often makes sense to bring in a backhoe or an auger to dig the footings. When you use excavating equipment, you can't dig the footings with the perimeter joists in place because you need room for the machinery. So take down the perimeter joists after you've laid out the footings on the ground, bring in the excavator, and dig the footings. When you're done, it's surprisingly easy to reinstall the perimeter joists, especially if you've been able to leave the goal-post-shaped supports in place (see pp. 125-127).

There are two other things to consider if you're building in a cold climate. The first is the concrete at the base of the posts. Where deep freeze occurs, the ground expands upward, or heaves. If the sides of the concrete are jagged—as they would be if you used the excavated hole as a form—the heaving soil might grab the sides of the concrete and lift the entire deck. It's good practice to use concrete tubes or build wood forms to create smooth sides when you pour concrete around the bottoms of the posts.

The other consideration is the height of the deck. Where heavy snow is expected, it makes sense to build the deck one step (7 in.) down from the top of the doorsill. This space makes it easier to open an outswinging door (usually a storm door) after a blizzard and keeps melting snow from seeping through the door opening.

Because building the deck at this height frequently places over half the band below the top of the foundation, there's a good chance you'll have to drill through the foundation to bolt the band to the house. If you're building a new house and you know where the deck will be, you can save yourself a lot of work by embedding these bolts as you build the foundation. Or, if you prefer, embed treated wood in the foundation to receive bolts when you install the band.

Post Layout

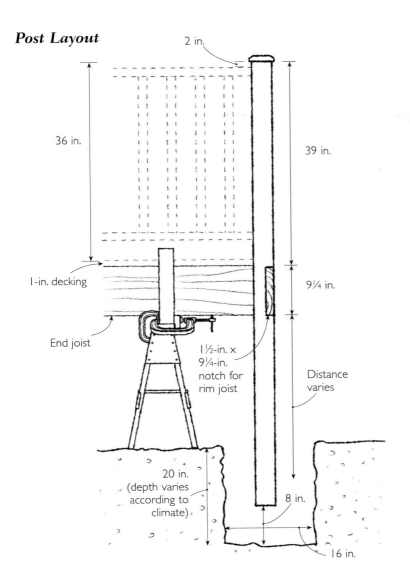

2 in.

36 in.

39 in.

1-in. decking

9¼ in.

End joist

1½-in. ×
9¼-in.
notch for
rim joist

Distance
varies

20 in.
(depth varies
according to
climate)

8 in.

16 in.

from the concrete. After years of
using this method, however, I'm
convinced that this moisture does
not threaten the structure (just
look at all the telephone poles that
have survived decades in the

ground). And there's a significant
advantage to encasing the posts
deep inside the concrete—the concrete weighs hundreds of pounds
and imparts a rock-solid rigidity to
the posts.

To get the posts set and the concrete poured in one fell swoop, I suspend each post above the bottom of the footing before I mix and pour the concrete. I begin this process by measuring the distance from the bottom of each footing to the underside of the perimeter joist. Then I subtract 8 in. from this dimension to allow for the 8 in. of concrete under the post that's required by my building code. After measuring and marking this distance on the post, I lay out a 1½-in. by 9¼-in. notch above the mark. There are two reasons I go to the trouble of making this notch. First, when I finish the deck, the perimeter joist(s) set in this notch bear directly on solid wood (instead of

relying entirely on the bolts for support). Second, this notch brings the outside face of the post—and thus the entire balustrade—even with the outside edge of the deck.

Once the notch is laid out, I measure and mark 39 in. above the top of the notch and cut the post off at that dimension. The 39-in. dimension provides for a rail that will be 36 in. above the top of the deck, which is required by code in my area. It also allows the post to project 2 in. above the rail (see the drawing on p. 133).

Next, I cut the post to length and cut out the notch, using a circular saw and sharp hand tools. Then I fit each post over the location laid out on the perimeter joists. When I get the post aligned with the layout, I clamp it to the joist and brace it plumb in both directions (see the drawing on the facing page). To make this task manageable, I often clamp a 2-ft. level to the post as I brace it plumb. Once the posts are plumb, I begin mixing concrete. With the bottom of the post suspended 8 in. above the bottom of the footing, I pour the concrete under and around the post until the footing is filled up to grade. To keep rainwater from pooling around the post, I build up the top surface of the concrete slightly and make it slope down and away from the post.

TRICKS OF THE TRADE

Cutting a Notch
To cut a 9¼-in. by 1½-in. notch in a 4x4 post, I set my circular saw blade to a depth of 1½ in. and don ear protection. After carefully cutting along the top and bottom lines of the layout, I quickly cut about two dozen kerfs between the first two cuts. Next I knock out the standing wafers of wood left between the kerfs with my hammer. I finish the job by paring the bottom of the notch smooth with a sharp chisel.

Installing Posts

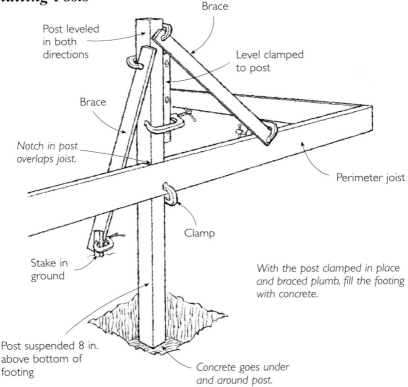

Brace

Post leveled in both directions

Level clamped to post

Brace

Notch in post overlaps joist.

Perimeter joist

Clamp

Stake in ground

With the post clamped in place and braced plumb, fill the footing with concrete.

Post suspended 8 in. above bottom of footing

Concrete goes under and around post.

Inside Joists

To avoid breaking the concrete, I allow it to cure for at least 72 hours before I resume work on the posts. When the cure period is over, I remove the clamp holding the post to the joist, drill ½-in. holes, and bolt the joist permanently to the post with carriage bolts. With the posts embedded in the concrete bases, the entire structure is now rigid. I no longer need the two diagonal braces to

hold the perimeter of the deck square. I remove the braces and I'm ready to install the rest of the joists.

The first thing I do is lay out the locations of the joists—a straightforward process. Pulling the tape from the same side of the deck, I measure and mark identical 16-in. on-center layouts on both the band and the rim joist. To measure the space between the band and the

Installing Inside Joists

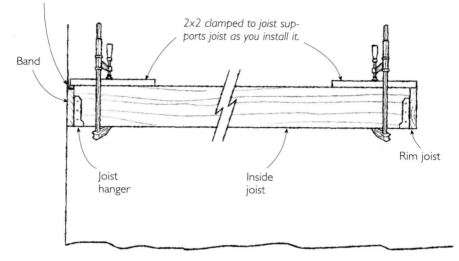

½-in. strip on top of band holds the joist ½ in. above band.

2x2 clamped to joist supports supports joist as you install it.

Band

Joist hanger

Inside joist

Rim joist

rim joist to determine how long to make the joists, I use a 1x2 strip as a measuring stick. Because there's no guarantee that the wall of the house is perfectly straight, I measure for each individual joist in the layout.

Once I've transferred the measurement to the joist, I cut it to length and install joist hangers on both ends. Before installing the joist hangers, however, I "crown" the joist. Most boards are slightly bowed, and you want to make sure the bow or crown of all the joists points up as they're installed. To crown each joist, I sight down the edge and mark the high side of the

bow with an arrow. Then, when I install the joist hangers, I note where the crown is and position the hanger with the seat on the opposite side of the board. This placement ensures that the joist will be oriented with the crown up when I install it.

After attaching hangers to both ends of the joist, I clamp a 2x2 block to the top of each end of the joist, with about 1 in. of the scrap projecting past the end of the joist (see the drawing above). I set a ½-in. strip of plywood on top of the band, then bring the joist inside the deck area and slide it into place between the band and the rim joist.

Four Ways to Straighten Deck Boards

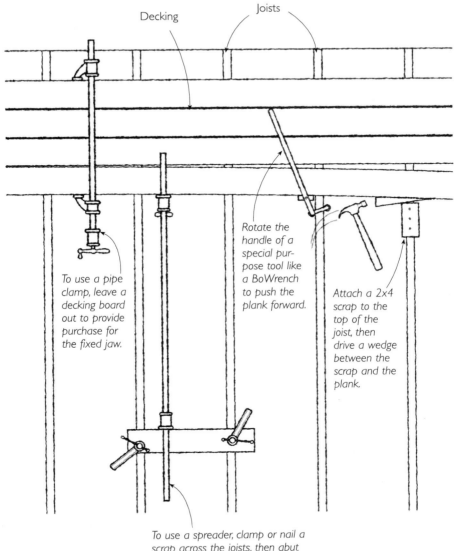

Decking

Joists

Rotate the handle of a special purpose tool like a BoWrench to push the plank forward.

To use a pipe clamp, leave a decking board out to provide purchase for the fixed jaw.

Attach a 2x4 scrap to the top of the joist, then drive a wedge between the scrap and the plank.

To use a spreader, clamp or nail a scrap across the joists, then abut the fixed jaw against the scrap as you propel the other jaw forward by turning the handle.

Installing the Stringer

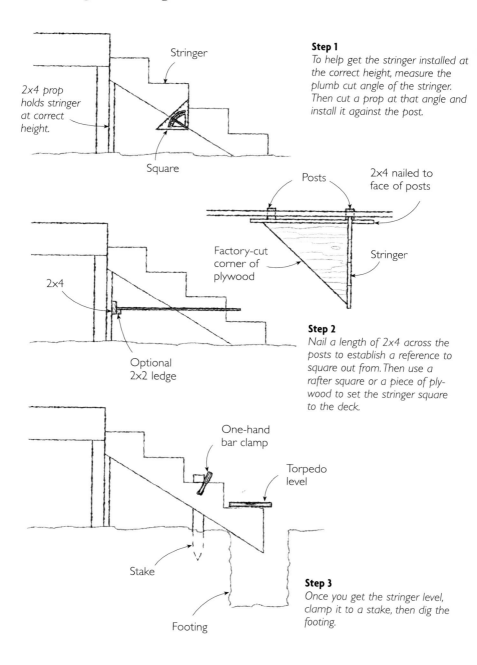

2x4 prop
holds stringer
at correct
height.

Stringer

Square

Step 1
To help get the stringer installed at the correct height, measure the plumb cut angle of the stringer. Then cut a prop at that angle and install it against the post.

Posts

2x4 nailed to face of posts

Factory-cut corner of plywood

Stringer

2x4

Optional 2x2 ledge

Step 2
Nail a length of 2x4 across the posts to establish a reference to square out from. Then use a rafter square or a piece of plywood to set the stringer square to the deck.

One-hand bar clamp

Torpedo level

Stake

Footing

Step 3
Once you get the stringer level, clamp it to a stake, then dig the footing.

The 2x2s hook over the band and the rim joist and hold the joist at the right height as I install it. The plywood strip holds the joist ½ in. above the band, but the other end of the joist sits flush to the rim joist. I attach the joist at the layout lines by driving nails through the flanges of the joist hangers.

Installing the Decking

Once I get all the joists installed, I start installing the decking. The main challenge is to force the wood—which is inevitably bowed and twisted—into a reasonably straight line as I install it. To do this, I use a BoWrench (see p. 41). There is also a similar tool called the Boardbender. If you don't have one of these special-purpose tools, you can use a pipe clamp, a spreader, or a block of wood and a wedge (see the drawing on p. 137). These techniques are not as fast as using a BoWrench or a Board-bender, but they get the job done.

Final Steps

The final steps for this deck are the latticework and the stairs and balustrade. Cutting and installing the sheets of lattice is a straight-forward task that shouldn't present problems for a solo builder. The design and layout of stairs, on the other hand, is a complicated task, but the only part that's challenging to do alone is installing the stringers. To install a stringer cor-rectly you have to do three things: attach it to the deck at the right height, install it square to the deck, and make the treads level.

To get the stringer at the right height, I nail or clamp a 2x4 prop against the post to hold the stringer up as I toe-nail it in place (Step 1 in the drawing on the facing page). Because the stairs slope at an angle, the top of the prop must be cut at the correct angle. The angle is the same as the plumb cut on the stringer and can be measured with a Stanley Quick Square or a Swanson Speed Square. (For most staircases, the angle is between 32° and 42°.) I sometimes incorpo-rate this prop into the design of the deck and leave it permanently in place.

To get the stringer square to the deck, start by temporarily installing a 2x4 across the posts (about halfway up). The 2x4 serves as a reference to square the stringer to. Most of the time, the stringers that run perpendicular to the deck are small and I can use a rafter square or the factory-cut corner of a sheet of plywood to get the stringer square to the 2x4 (Step 2). When I have to build a long set of stairs off a high deck, I usually design the deck so that the stairs run along the side of the deck or the house. That way the stairs don't project deeply and awkwardly into the yard. On the rare occasion when I have to square up a long stringer to the deck, I fabricate a large right triangle out of straight strips of wood and use it instead of the square or sheet of plywood to set the stringer square to the 2x4.

To get the treads of the stringer level, I drive a stake into the ground alongside the stringer and about 20 in. in from the bottom end. Then I set a torpedo level on a tread and raise the stringer until I get a level reading (Step 3 in the drawing on p. 138). When the tread is level, I clamp the stringer to the stake with a one-hand bar clamp. With the top of the stringer nailed in place and the bottom clamped to the stake, I dig a foot-

ing under the bottom of the stringer and pour concrete under and around the stringer. If you use this method, make sure you use wood for the stringers that's rated for ground contact.

The final step is to fabricate and install the sections of the balustrade. The fabrication of these sections is not a difficult job (assuming you have the required carpentry skills). The only tricky part when you're working alone is to hold it at the right height as you install it. I usually rest the section on a couple of 2x4 blocks (which I've set on edge). The blocks hold the bottom rail of the balustrade $3\frac{1}{2}$ in. off the deck. This height looks good and allows the homeowner to sweep leaves under the rail.

T he wide selection of portable equipment available today makes it possible for one person working alone to build an entire house. But there's a difference between what's possible and what's practical. Some things are too expensive, too risky, or simply too much bother to do alone. In this chapter, I'll identify the jobs that I can't, or won't, do by myself.

The selection of jobs has been shaped to a large degree by my skills and temperament, but this selection might not be right for you. To help you decide, I'll explain how I weigh the risks of doing these tasks solo. Then I'll explain why and when I bring in help for those jobs. I'll also discuss the mental challenges of facing the workday alone and how I deal with them.

Jobs for More Than One

There are several jobs that I can't do—either because I don't have the necessary skills or because I don't have the required licenses. There are other jobs that I can do but would rather farm out to others. And then there are the jobs that I do by myself on some occasions but bring in reinforcements or hire out to subcontractors on others. My schedule, the schedule of subcontractors, costs, and the scope of the job all enter into the decision. Underlying all of these issues, though, is the simple question: "Is doing this job myself really worth the time and effort?" Sometimes it isn't.

Laying Out the Foundation of a Whole House

In chapter 2, I described the layout of the foundation for a fairly large addition. Adding just a few feet to the length and width of that foundation would make it large enough for a small house. Yet, even for a small house foundation, I usually line up a helper for the layout. What makes me decide to bring in a helper for the house foundation? The main problem is not the size of the house foundation but the lack of solid surfaces from which to pull measurements.

When you lay out the foundation for an addition, you can pull most of your measurements off the existing house. When you lay out the foundation for a house, on the other hand, there are no solid surfaces on which to anchor your tape measure. It's possible to set up brackets for every measurement, but it's more cost-effective to line up a helper to hold the end of the tape. For a simple, rectangular foundation, these measurements can be completed in less than an hour.

Pouring Concrete

When it comes to concrete, time is of the essence. First, the material itself has a time limit. As soon as water hits the dry ingredients of concrete a chemical reaction called hydration begins. This reaction causes the ingredients to coalesce and harden. It is a relentless and irreversible process that can progress at an alarming pace. On hot summer days, the mushy mixture that flows down the chute of a concrete truck becomes rock-hard in a matter of hours. Needless to say, it's essential to get the concrete placed and finished before that happens.

The second thing that makes time so important is the way concrete is produced and supplied. The cheapest and most efficient way to install concrete in quantities exceeding 1 cu. yd. is to buy "ready-mixed" concrete. This material is delivered in the large mixing trucks that are a familiar sight on American roads. The heavy equipment used to make and haul concrete is expensive, and the suppliers who have invested in this equipment cannot afford to have it tied up by ill-prepared contractors. To encourage builders to be ready for their trucks, suppliers stipulate the amount of time the customer may use to unload the material. Usually the supplier allows 7 to 10 minutes per yard of concrete. Builders who exceed those limits have to pay more.

Getting the concrete unloaded, placed, and finished as quickly as possible is extremely important, but it can be very difficult to do. One cubic yard of concrete weighs close to 4,000 lb., and residential jobs often require several yards of concrete. (For example, a poured basement usually requires over 20 yd. of concrete.) Rolling the concrete into position in wheelbarrows, dumping it, pulling it into place, leveling it, and going over it with a float is grueling work. It's just about impossible for one person to pour and finish a large amount of concrete.

Even on fairly small pours of 2 yd. or 3 yd., which I might well be able to handle by myself, I don't gamble that everything will go according to plan. Sometimes, for example, the truck can't get as close to the pour

as I had hoped. Even worse, the truck might get stuck or the form might fail. Being undermanned during these moments is a prescription for a messy and expensive fiasco. There's no stopping and there's no turning back in the middle of a concrete pour, and I would much rather err on the side of caution. I always have plenty of help when a concrete truck rumbles up to one of my jobs. Even when things go well, there's plenty of work for everyone.

When I have small amounts of concrete to pour—for the footings of a deck, for example—I buy bags of dry concrete and mix it myself using my portable mixer. As a rule, I mix my own concrete and work alone on jobs that require less than 1 cu. yd. of concrete. But on anything larger, I buy ready-mix and schedule a crew to meet the truck.

Setting Trusses

Trusses are difficult for one person to install. They're long, broad, and sometimes quite heavy. On top of that, they have to be handled properly. A truss should be carried vertically—not in a flat position— and every effort should be made to avoid bending it excessively. Allowing a truss to sag and bend loosens the connecting plates and jeopardizes the structural integrity of the truss. Because of these difficulties, I rarely use trusses. Even on small jobs that require only small, easy-to-handle trusses, I prefer to stick-build the roof. For me, laying out and building a stick-built roof is easier (and more enjoyable) than going through the rigmarole of ordering trusses, storing them on site, and installing them.

Sometimes, though, trusses are specified for the job and I have to use them. Typically these trusses are specified because they can span wide-open spaces. Consequently, they're almost always too big for me to hoist and install alone. I could hire a crane to help lift the trusses into place, but the cost of the crane would mount considerably as I slowly installed the trusses by myself. It's more cost-effective to line up a carpentry crew for setting trusses. When very large trusses are specified, it makes sense to bring in a carpentry crew and hire a crane.

Installing Large Window and Door Units

Like trusses, window and door units have to be handled with care. After you remove the straps and cardboard that they're shipped in, the units are pretty fragile. For this reason, I never use a mechanical hoist to help lift them in place as I install them. Besides, the cost of setting up such an apparatus exceeds the cost of getting a couple of carpenters on site for an hour or so to help me set the unit.

Some large sliding-glass doors arrive in pieces and are easy to install solo. The easy, piece-by-piece approach raises the question: Is it worthwhile to take out the glass panels that come in pre-assembled sliding glass doors or French door units so they can be installed solo? For that matter, does it make sense to lighten large windows by removing the sash? I don't think so. Taking the units apart would create a lot of work. It's easier to schedule a crew to help install the window and door units.

Scheduling a crew for this task rarely causes delays. When I finish the frame, there are usually several jobs that I can do in the meanwhile, including finishing eaves and rakes, installing roof shingles, and framing interior walls. This makes it easy to defer the window and door installation until another carpenter or a carpentry crew finds an hour or two to help me out. (Some of the larger units I've installed have required every bit of a four-man crew to muscle them into place.)

As I mentioned in chapter 6, I install any unit that I can lift into place by myself. I often install all the units I can, therefore, and save the large, heavy units for a day when I have some help. Sometimes, though, when I manage to get a crew on site immediately, it makes sense to use them to get all the windows and doors installed at once.

Using Subcontractors to Finish the Job

After I get the frame built, I turn increasingly to subcontractors to help me finish the job. There are several reasons I look to others for help. First, I have to use licensed contractors for the electrical, plumbing, and HVAC (heating, venting, and air conditioning). The truth is I would use these subcontractors even if I were not required by law to do so. I have no training in those trades and don't have the tools or expertise. I'm happy to turn that work over to licensed specialists.

Second, as the materials that cover the inside and outside of the frame become increasingly specialized so do the tools and skills required to install them. A dizzying variety of materials is now available to cover the inside surfaces of a house. Some materials are so unique that the manufacturer sells them only through certified installers. There are a number of these specialized jobs that I don't do for different reasons. Floor coverings vary greatly, for example, and I routinely sub-out the installation.

I've never installed carpet or hardwood flooring, and I've rarely put down vinyl flooring (if I do, it's always a small sheet with no seams). I've fabricated plastic-laminate countertops on site, but the unforgiving nature of plastic laminates causes stress and I'd just as soon farm out the fumes and the stress to someone else. And after cracking two custom-made panels of insulated glass on the same ill-fated Friday, I now pay my glass company to send a glazier out to my job when I need to install fixed panes of glass.

The third reason I turn to subcontractors is that they are willing and prepared to do jobs I dislike. I sometimes hire out the insulation work just to avoid a day or two of itchy, unpleasant work. In a similar vein, I sub-out the painting for all but the smallest jobs, partly because I hate to paint and partly because I don't have the skills of a first-rate painter.

A final reason I turn to subcontractors at this stage in the job is time and exhaustion. At this point, I'm ready to finish and so is my client. Skilled subcontractors can often knock out the finishing touches much faster than I can without sacrificing quality. I like to hang and finish drywall, for example, and I do a pretty good job on small to medium-sized additions. But when I have a lot of drywall to hang and finish, I bring in a drywall contractor to speed up the job.

Facing the Workday Alone

For many people, the hardest part of working alone is spending the day laboring in solitude. I enjoy the benefits of working alone, but it does present some mental challenges that are different from the obvious physical challenges mentioned throughout the book. Here, I'll address those challenges and tell you the ways I've found to cope with them, and even to view them positively.

Making Decisions Solo

One thing that's missing when you work alone is an informal consultant. You can't bounce ideas off coworkers or have them "edit" your layouts. You have to make every decision, deal with all the clients, inspectors, and suppliers, and, of course, do all the building. You're the boss—and the crew. These responsibilities can bring a lot of stress. The key to combating the stress is to develop confidence in your skills as a builder. There is no quick way to do this, just the slow way—through experience. The more I work by myself successfully, the less stressful it is for me to make all the decisions.

Once you get used to the decision making, though, it can be hard to work for someone else. When I've worked for other contractors, I've often found it frustrating and demoralizing to defer to someone else. When I work alone, I have complete control over the job and over my day.

Another benefit to making all the decisions is the lack of controversy. On construction sites, arguments over the fastest way to do a job often take more time than any of the methods being debated. Workers also argue over the level of quality that's acceptable, what station the radio should be tuned into, and who is working hard and being productive. When you work alone, these interpersonal tensions are blessedly nonexistent.

Getting Motivated

Staying enthused about your work can be hard when you're alone. When you work for or with someone else, that person can help you get motivated. There are all kinds of ways this works: The boss might offer a reward or threaten punishment; coworkers sometimes stimulate by providing competition or peer pressure. When you work alone, on the other hand, you have no one to motivate you and you have every opportunity to goof off. For craftsmen who like the excite-

Mapping Out the Day's Work

The first tools I use every morning are a pen and a piece of paper. Over coffee, I do a full day's work in my mind, jotting down the tools and materials I'll need and roughing out a schedule for the day. Perhaps the most important part of this list is the "bring from home" category. Few things are more frustrating than having the perfect tool or jig sitting on a shelf at home when you need it on the job.

As I envision what I'll be doing that day, I write down the tools, jigs, brackets, and materials that I'll need to bring from home. Then I cross these items off my list as I load them on my truck. For some jobs, like hanging a door, I've developed a standard checklist (shown at right), which I have filed and ready to use. If I have to pick up materials and supplies, I create other categories, like "lumberyard" and "tile store," with a list of the supplies I'll need.

I also write down a battle plan for the day's work. Sometimes my plan for the day is straightforward. As you've seen throughout this book, the sequence for the day's work is often dictated by the work itself.

This isn't always the case. At many points in the job, particularly after I've got the frame of a house or addition built, there's no set sequence. At these points, there may be numerous loose ends that I need to take care of, as well as a variety of jobs that I can begin. That's when making a punch list of the individual jobs helps to keep me from being overwhelmed by the overall project.

In spite of my best efforts, I sometimes forget an important tool, a piece of hardware, or some other item. To remember these, I jot them down as I work and incorporate them into my list the next morning.

Checklist for hanging a door

- Screwdrivers
- All-purpose brackets
- Drills, drill bits
- Door-boring jig
- Edge tools
- Circular saw
- Cutting guides
- Sawhorses
- Three-way cord
- Router, router bits
- Hinge-mortising template
- Clamps

ment of working in a crew, driving relentlessly forward, seeing dramatic changes in a few hours, a day alone on a construction site would be excruciatingly boring.

To keep from being bored, I bring a radio to work. That way there's always some background noise, and I don't feel completely alone. The radio also allows me to follow a sporting event, a discussion, or a piece of music while I'm busy building.

Keeping motivated on large jobs, when it feels like I'll never finish, is possibly the biggest challenge. To avoid getting discouraged in the middle of such jobs, I set daily goals and try not to focus too hard on the finished product. I begin the day by writing down what I want to achieve (see the sidebar on p. 147). This keeps me on track and gives me a sense of accomplishment when I can cross something off the list. If I hit the doldrums during the day, I start doing the easiest things on the list—just to keep moving forward. I often catch a second wind in the course of knocking out these items, then take on the harder tasks with newfound energy.

Because I genuinely like my job, I usually have little trouble drumming up enthusiasm for my day's work. All these tips won't help you keep motivated, though, if you don't like your job.

Dealing with the Solitude

A final difficulty some people have with working alone is the solitude. Having no coworkers means there's no one to spice up the day with conversation. There are no jokes and no laughter. There's no one to commiserate with when the weather's bad or when you have to do an unpleasant job. There's none of the camaraderie that often pervades construction sites.

These are things I sometimes miss. At the same time, I haven't forgotten that coworkers aren't always fun and charming. I recall a few that made the day seem long. Working with others, I've found, can be a lot of fun or it can be stressful; usually it's a combination of the two. When you work alone, you don't have the fun or the stress; you have the quiet. There are no techniques for dealing with it. It's something that grows on you.

Resources

Some of the tools listed throughout the book can be found in local hardware and building supply stores, but most have to be ordered directly from the manufacturer or through a catalog.

Hoists and Jacks

Lightning Tool Corporation
10711 Evergreen Way Suite A
Everett, WA 98204
(888) 839-5237
(206) 440-0981 (fax)
http://www.lightningtool.com
Manufacturer of Lightning Lift

Patterson Avenue Tool Co., Inc.
6515 High Meadow Court
Long Grove, IL 60047
(800) 662-3557
(847) 949-8149 (fax)
http://www.tjak.com
Manufacturer of T-Jak

Proctor Products Co., Inc.
P. O. Box 697
Kirkland, WA 98083-0697
(425) 822-9296
(206) 634-2396 (fax)
http://www.proctorp.com
Manufacturer of Proctor Wall Jacks

Telpro, Inc.
Route 1, Box 138
Grand Forks, ND 58201
(800) 441-0551
http://www.telproinc.com
Manufacturer of Panel-Lift

Levers, Clamps, and Spreaders

Cepco Tool Co.
P.O. Box 153
Spencer, NY 14883
(800) 466-9626
Manufacturer of BoWrench

Mayhew Tools
2 Sears Street, P.O. Box 68
Shelburne Falls, MA 01370
(800) 872-0037
http://www.mayhew.com
Manufacturer of the Tweaker

James Morton /American Clamping
50 Franklin Street, P.O. Box 399
Batavia, NY 14021
(716) 344-0025
http://www.jamesmorton.com
Distributor of Bessey Clamps (the Bessey Powergrip is the best one-hand bar clamp on the market)

Wade Mfg. Co.
P.O. Box 23666
Portland, OR 97223
(503) 692-5353
(503) 692-5358 (fax)
Manufacturer of Mastodon Jaw Extenders

Measuring and Marking Tools

General Tools
80 White Street,
New York, NY 10013
(212) 431-6100
Manufacturer of No. 523 adjustable trammel points (the best trammel points for construction layout)

Laser Tools Co.
3520 W. 69th Street, Suite 401
Little Rock, AR 72209
(800) 598-5973
Manufacturer of laser levels

The Stanley Works
1000 Stanley Drive
New Britain, CT 06053
(800) 782-6539
www.stanleyworks.com
Manufacturer of the Stanley Quick
Square

Swanson Tool Co.
1010 Lambrecht Road
Frankfort, IL 60423
(815) 469-9453
Manufacturer of Swanson Speed
Square and Swanson Mag Square

Tool Catalogs

Garrett Wade Tool Company
161 Avenue of the Americas
New York, NY 10013
(800) 221-2942
(800) 566-9525 (fax)
http://www.garrettwade.com

Highland Hardware
1045 N. Highland Ave., NE
Atlanta, GA 30306
(404) 872-4466
(404) 876-1941 (fax)
http://www.highland-hardware.com

Tool Crib of the North
1550 S. 48th Street, Suite 100
Grand Forks, ND 58201
(800) 358-3096
(800) 343-4205 (fax)
http://www.toolcribofthenorth.com

Trend-Lines
135 American Legion Highway
Revere, MA 02151
(800) 767-9999
http://www.trend-lines.com

William Alden Company
P.O. Box 4005
Taunton, MA 02780
(800) 249-8665
http://www.williamalden.com

Woodworker's Supply of North
Carolina
1125 Jay Lane
Graham, NC 27253
(800) 645-9292

Building Guides

Bailey, Robert F. *The Pocket Size
Carpenter's Helper*. Liberty, ME: R.S.
Wood Inc., 1986.

Byrne, Michael. *Setting Tile*. Newtown,
CT: The Taunton Press, 1995.

Carroll, John. *Measuring, Marking &
Layout: A Builder's Guide*. Newtown,
CT: The Taunton Press, 1998.

Kreh, Richard. *Building with Masonry:
Brick, Block & Concrete*. Newtown,
CT: The Taunton Press, 1998.

Schuttner, Scott. *Building and
Designing Decks*. Newtown, CT: The
Taunton Press, 1993.

Wagner, John D. *House Framing*.
Upper Saddle River, N.J.: Creative
Homeowner Press, 1998.

Index

B

Barge rafters. *See* Rafters, barge.
Brackets:
 all-purpose, 51-52, 89, 102, 103, 122
 for holding siding, 97
 L-shaped, 24-25, 29, 31
 steel, for installing sheathing, 50-51
 U-shaped, 109

C

Cabinets, wall, hanging, 110, 111
Chair rail, installing, 106-108
Chalk box, modified, using, 83, 85, 96
Clamps:
 bar, 11-12, 43
 C-, 11, 12
 pipe, 11, 12
 types of, 10-12
Compass, beam, for tile layout, 115-16
Crown molding, installing, 106-108

D

Decimals, converting to fractions, 28
Decking, plywood, installing, 39-41, 42
Decks:
 balustrade, installing, 140
 band joist,
  installing, 122-23
  laying out, 119, 122
 in cold climates, 132
 decking,
  installing, 139
  straightening, 137
 end joists,
  installing, 125-27
  squaring, 127-29
 flashing for, 123-25
 footings for, 131, 134
 inside joists, installing, 135-36
 large, laying out, 130
 lattice, installing, 139
 laying out, on house, 118-19
 posts,
  installing, 131, 133-35
  laying out, 130-31, 133
 rim joists, installing, 127, 128
 safety and, 123
 stairs, installing, 138, 139-40
 types of, 120-21
Doors:
 door-knob hole in, enlarging, 102
 installing, 88, 90-91, 144-45
 support brackets for, 102, 103
Drywall, hanging, 99-103, 145-46
 lift for, 100, 101-103
 measuring sticks with, 100-101

E

Eaves:
 frames of, 85-86
 scaffolding for, 82-83
 See also Fascia. Rakes. Soffit.

F

Fascia, installing, 7, 86-87, 88
Fastening boards, technique for, 13-14
Floors, framing, 37-41
Flue liners, installing, 20
Foundations:
 help with, need for, 142
 laying out, 19-32

J

Joists, floor:
 laying out, 38, 39
 straightening, 39
 See also Decks.

L

Ladders, commercial-grade, 13
Laser levels, for foundation layout, 21, 22-23
Lumber, straightening, 39, 42-43

M

Masonry structures:
 squaring up, 32-33
 See also Foundations.
Math, and the solo builder, 26
 See also Pythagorean Theorem.
Measuring sticks:
 for drywall layout, 100-101
 for installing trim, 104-106
 for rafter layout, 67-68
 vs. tape measures, 14
 for tile layout, 112, 115
 using, 16-17

Mortar, working with, 19-20
Mudsills:
    anchor bolt layout on, 37-38
    joist layout on, 38, 39

P

Plumb bobs:
    threading, 78
    using, 72, 73, 79-80
Pythagorean Theorem:
    and deck layout, 127-28
    and foundation layout, 27-28
    and roof layout, 62-63
    and tile layout, 112

R

Rafters:
    barge, installing, 83, 85
    geometry of, 62-63
    installing, 74-75
    laying out, 63-68
        jig for, 63-64
        measuring stick for, 67-68
    layout systems for, 60
Rakes:
    building, 84
    rake board, installing, 87
    scaffolding for, 82-83
    See also Eaves. Rafters, barge.
Ridge beams:
    cutting, 70-72, 74
    raising, 68-70
Roofs:
    building, 68-76
    deck of, installing, 75-76
    laying out, 58-68
        math vs. nonmath approach, 58
    pitch of, converting to degrees, 74
    shingling, 91-93
    stick-built, vs. truss, 58, 59
    truss, 57, 59, 144
    See also Rafters. Ridge beams.

S

Safety:
    and cutting trim, 103
    and raising ridge beam, 70
    and raising walls, 44
    and working alone, 6
Sawhorses, building, 53

Scaffolding:
    pipe, 12-13
    for roof construction, 69-70, 75
    setting up, 33-35, 82-83
Siding, wood, installing, 93-97
Soffit, installing, 88
Spreaders, described, 12, 39, 40
Studs, wall, installing, 82
Subcontractors, need for, 99, 145-46
Subfascia:
    installing, 75-76, 83
    See also Fascia.

T

Tiles, laying out, 112-16
Tools:
    hand, value of, 8
    joist-straightening, 39, 40
    manufactured, versatility of, 9
    special-purpose/site-built, 16-17
Top plates, laying out, 79-82
Trim:
    cutting, 103
    installing, 106-108
    measuring walls for, 103-106
    See also Chair rail. Crown molding.
Trusses:
    help with, need for, 143-44
    See also Roofs.
Turnbuckles, choosing, 49

W

Walls, bearing:
    erecting, 43-45
    laying out, 41-42
    plumbing, 52, 54
    sheathing, 50-52
    squaring, 46-50
    straightening, 52, 54-56
Walls, nonbearing, framing, 78-82
Windows:
    help with, need for, 144-45
    installing, 88, 89-90
Workbench, job-site, 54
Working alone:
    challenges of, 6-10
    limitations of, 142-46
    and motivation, 146, 148
    and planning, 8, 10, 147
    rewards of, 3, 148
    and solitude, dealing with, 146, 148